CHILDREN OF REFUGEES

CHILDREN OF REFUGEES
Torture, Human Rights, and Psychological Consequences

Aida Alayarian

KARNAC

First published in 2017 by
Karnac Books Ltd
118 Finchley Road
London NW3 5HT

British Library Cataloguing in Publication Data

A C.I.P. for this book is available from the British Library

ISBN-13: 978-1-78220-298-1

Typeset by Medlar Publishing Solutions Pvt Ltd, India

Printed in Great Britain

www.karnacbooks.com

Safeguarding children and young people is a
responsibility for all of society
(Children Act 2004)

CONTENTS

ACKNOWLEDGEMENTS

The existence of this book could not have been achieved without the fantastic support from Karnac publishing and of course with valuable and priceless combination of stimulus insight that I have gained from the children and young people that I have been privileged to work with and to understand and able to relate to their issue, to read and follow the rules and regulations affected their life and their psychological being. It goes without saying that no work can be accomplished without the guidance of experts in the field and again I feel privileged to have had some of the best to help me to transfer my ideas into a product. I owe this satisfaction to many of my good colleagues, friends, and family for their insight in discussion and for guidance, understanding, and their imparting the knowledge, whenever required, and for sympathetic tolerant with me when I could not clearly conceptualise my ways of thinking. I would like to express my greatest gratitude to the children and families who have helped me to work with them to discover their story and being able to go through a challenging journey they had to face. I would also like to thank many of the wonderful colleagues who supported me throughout this work for many years. I am grateful to Josephine Klein, Lennox Thomas, John Denford, and Micol Ascoli for their continuous support; for their wisdom; for their constant approval and encouragements that provide me with confidence to work in the area I felt is neglected so far in our field of work. I wish to thank David Armstrong for his undivided support and interest that inspired me and encouraged me to go my own way for the interest of the beneficiaries of the children, young people, and family of refugees and asylum seekers at the Refugee Therapy Centre. Last but not the least I want to thank Oliver Rathbone and Rod Tweedy and everyone at Karnac Books, who have made this book possible.

ABOUT THE AUTHOR

Aida Alayarian is a consultant clinical psychologist, child psycho-therapist since 1986, and adult psychoanalytic psychotherapist since 1998. She has a Masters in Medical Anthropology and Intercultural Psychotherapy, with a background in Medicine. She is the founder and currently Clinical Director of the Refugee Therapy Centre.

FOREWORD

The world is watching a crisis of unprecedented scale unfold. In every region of the world, women and men are on the move, most of them fleeing from war, violence, persecution, torture, poverty, discrimination, and exclusion. Oftentimes, they are fleeing from a combination of these, or while fleeing they face a compounded combination of these. The motivation to move includes the hope of receiving international protection, the search for better odds at living or for building a better life, or the intent to create an opportunity for the family to achieve these goals through family reunification.

According to estimates of the United Nations High Commissioner for Refugees, half of the people on the move today are children,[1] and within the global flows, international and regional bodies have documented extraordinary increases in the number of unaccompanied children.[2]

While the motivation to move is manifold, the combined experience of reception and assessment institutions leads to the working theory that great proportions of persons on the move have been subjected to torture or cruel, inhuman or degrading treatment or punishment in the country of origin. Furthermore, as a result of the extreme risk to which people on the move are exposed, a significant proportion of those who were not victims at the origin will be victimised during their travels.

In particular, the movement of children greatly increases vulnerability to abuse, violence, and mistreatment by state and non-state authorities, smugglers, and traffickers.

The complexity of this problematic is compounded by the gaps in widespread knowledge and understanding of the delicate and complex needs of persons subjected to torture or ill treatment. In transit or receiving countries, centres that provide health-based rehabilitation are in the forefront of this struggle. Yet, to see any of these centres be provided with resources adequate to face the enormity of their mission is as rare nowadays as is to hear responsible political discourse concerning the issue of refugees, asylum seekers, and migrants

In this book Dr Aida Alayarian makes a significant contribution to the unpostponable work of addressing these challenges, an invaluable contribution in the context of scarcity in which all members of the torture rehabilitation sector work. Taking point of departure in the holistic approach that is the trademark of the movement for full implementation of the right to rehabilitation, theoretical and clinical dimensions of the needs of children on the move are explored, as are the legal and clinical tools to satisfy them, and the political and practical measures required to make possible the functioning of these tools.

Dr Alayarian's work reaches far and wide, and this book is a significant collection of her reflections concerning concepts crucial in the fight against torture, such as the nature of the rule of law, the work against impunity and the social determinants of inequality and discrimination. In particular, the text is exceptionally sharp at identifying the manner in which different layers of discrimination and violence interact to knit the impenetrable fabric of exclusion that separates migrant, asylum seeker and refugee children from the resources required to nurture their full potential. In particular, the second part of the book presents case studies and narratives of how the challenges faced by children on the move are exponentially increased when combined with the stigma of mental health.

Yet, this exploration does not rest only upon an academic base: chapter after chapter the reader will be exposed to first-hand accounts of concern for the troubles of the men and women who pas every day through the offices of the Refugee Therapy Centre in London. These testimonies serve as a sort of Ariadne's thread to maintain the reader's focus on the crucial matter under question: in the words of Dr Alayarian, how to: "Create a world where all children and young people are respected, valued and heard [...]. Our collective thinking and action and our general objectives should include our conviction that childhood should be happy for all children in the world regardless of their ethnicity, race, class, colour and cultural outlook; that all young people deserve to reach their full potential; and that refugee children should be provided the support they need to become good members of society."

The movement for the effective implementation of right to rehabilitation, of which the Refugee Therapy Centre and the International Council for the Rehabilitation for Torture Victims are part, will find many of its political claims fulfilled when children have complete access to "as full rehabilitation as possible" in the terms of Article 14 of the United Nations Convention Against Torture and Other Cruel, Inhuman and Degrading Treatment or Punishment. The thoughtful work of Dr Alayarian is a clear contribution to showing concrete ways to reach this objective.

Victor Madrigal-Borloz
Secretary-General
International Rehabilitation Council
for Torture Victims
Escazú, Costa Rica

Notes

1. Globally, children below the age of eighteen constituted fifty-one per cent of the refugee population in 2014 (UNHCR, Statistical Yearbook 2014, p. 50).
2. In 2014, authorities in the United States of America reported having apprehended almost 70,000 unaccompanied children (Inter-American Commission on Human Rights; Human rights situation of refugee and migrant families and unaccompanied children in the United States of America. OEA/Ser. L/V/II. 155 Doc. 16, p. 9.)

INTRODUCTION

"The support and protection of children cannot be achieved by a single agency... every service has to play its part. All staff must have placed upon them the clear expectation that their primary responsibility is to the child and his or her family."
—Lord Laming, Victoria Climbié Inquiry Report, 2003

It is generally believed that we live in a multi-cultural society where diversity and difference are understood and encouraged. Interpretation on this view signals a culture of civilisation with humanity and social order in conjunction with the intention that society consists of individuals getting together and representing different interest groups; a society where people can exercise their rights regardless of class, gender, race or any other distinguishing characteristics. This book focuses on important matter of human right to see whether we are far from being such a society, although this is often assumed by some newly arrived refugees who have escaped persecutions, discrimination and torture in their home country. Such expectations cause disappointment for many newly arrived young refugees who have endured torture and human right violations and who are seeking safety. This can contribute to further stress and psychological problems. This is especially relevant for those who already suffer with mental health issues, as these difficulties and worries are not adequately shared and understood by people in the host country. There is also the reality of intentional and unintentional neglect of and discrimination against children and young people of refugees and other migrants through denial of social and cultural differences, as well as lack of consideration and compassion from decision makers that is directly affecting appropriate services for refugees. Littlewood and Lipsedge (1989) argued that situations in which identity is ambiguous can steer and proceed to the alienated elucidation of paranoia or of religion, but people may also generate an identity which lies outside the ambiguous options and which can transcend them.

Torture is a strategic means of limiting, controlling, and repressing basic human rights of individuals and communities that is often covert and denied by authorities. Deliberate infliction of pain and suffering or intimidation or coercion on children to obtain a confession or information, for punishment of real or perceived offences on the basis of discrimination about race, ethnic or political affiliation, is practiced in many places around the world. Impact of torture on children may vary depending on the child's coping strategies, cultural and social circumstances. As clinicians while our main objective is provision of therapeutic intervention, our focus is also need to influence policy and practice by researching for evidence and demonstrating solutions to improve the lives, homes and communities of children disadvantaged by torture and the services that support them. We need to seek to provide some remedies to children of refugees who are suffering the consequence of trauma they have endured. In this book I will give a brief introduction of the work at the Refugee Therapy Centre. I shall discuss and reflect on children and torture. I will present a vignette and some examples of children tortured and the need of clinical intervention as well as other services to help children and young people coping with practical issues related to the processes of asylum-seeking process, adaptation, integration and resettlement.

Children are supposed to play, to laugh, to look forward to their future and have hope; and above all to be a child. They are not supposed to be abused for food, chained to a wall or be in any way tortured. They need care and protection. With the recent flood of refugee and immigrations, it is not acceptable to simply watch the way children are treated in Europe, indeed around the world; we have a social responsibility to say loudly and repeatedly torturing children is wrong. Children torture remains widespread in the world including Afghanistan, Algeria, Angola, Brazil, Burundi, China, Colombia, Democratic Republic of the Congo, Ecuador, Eritrea, Ethiopia, Georgia, Honduras, Iran, Iraq, Israel/occupied territories, Lebanon, Mexico, Moldova, Mongolia, Nepal, Paraguay, Saudi Arabia, Serbia, Sri Lanka, South Africa, Sudan, Swaziland, and many others. The largest group of tortured children are amongst refugees. We need to act to put a stop to this and save children from torture. There are high numbers of unaccompanied children, mainly coming from Latin America, Africa, and the Middle-East, amongst them, child soldiers, those affected by armed conflict street violence, living in extreme poverty, abandonment and child labour. Monitoring the violation of children's rights should be encouraged and commissioned to be carried out by the local, regional and international humanitarian and rehabilitation organisations. As clinicians, we must also affirm a commitment to protect people's basic human rights, indeed rights of children. Many refugee children that I have worked with suffered appalling violence and have been tortured as part of collective punishments for whole communities, or as a means of extracting information from parents. Some children are exposed to physical, mental and emotional abuse and torture and suffer immeasurable pain. In some countries children are tortured as a form of punishment for their parents, whilst in others children are as likely as adults to be captured, imprisoned and subject to torture. In some Asian, Latin American and African countries such as Congo or Rwanda, for the first time in history children have been imprisoned and are facing trial for genocide. Child imprisonment and ill treatment is therefore an increasing concern. Sexual violence is particularly common in these ethnic conflicts. In Afghanistan, Rwanda or the Balkans, girls suffered the added trauma of sexual abuse and rape, which can be the most intrusive memory that these girls carry into their adult lives. In Bosnia and Herzegovina and Croatia, and indeed in Rwanda it has been deliberate policy to rape teenage girls and force them to bear "the enemy's child". Moreover, in Rwanda rape has been systematically used as a weapon of ethnic cleansing to destroy community ties. Many of young girls who became pregnant were then ostracised by their own families and community; some abandoned their babies, some committed suicide, and some kept their enemy's child, at the expense of losing relationships with all other family members. Many tortured children have lived in circumstances that most of us could never imagine. There are disturbing incidents, such as the one in the Renamo camps in Mozambique, where young boys, who themselves had been traumatised by violence, frequently inflicted sexual violence on young girls. No child should be chained to a wall and be raped as these girls were, and no child should be raped. Even girls who are not forcibly raped may still be obliged to trade sexual favours for food, shelter or physical protection for themselves, their baby or younger siblings. The rise of sexual abuse increases the sexually transmitted diseases particularly of HIV/AIDS. One of the common factors contributing to the high rates of AIDS is that some girls had to trade sex for security during the country's civil war and some of these girls suffer the consequence of such a torture to the end of their life.

European states abolished torture from their statutory law in the late eighteenth and early nineteenth centuries. England abolished torture in about 1640, Scotland in 1708, Denmark around 1770, Russia in 1774, Austria and Polish-Lithuanian Commonwealth in 1776, Italy in 1786, France in 1789, Sweden in 1722, the Netherlands in 1798, Spain, the Napoleonic conquest in 1808, Norway in 1819 and Portugal in 1826. The last European jurisdictions to abolish legal torture were Portugal in 1828 and Switzerland in 1851. However, we are far away from a world without torture.

Torture is a detestable crime under any circumstances. But the need for action is particularly critical when it is committed against children. And the stark reality is that although we do not often hear much about it, each day countless children are targets of torture or affected by the torture of a loved one. The absolute prohibition of torture is specifically mentioned in the UN Convention on the Rights of the Child. But whilst the question of violence against children is increasingly debated and attended to globally, generally there is little focus on and awareness about the specific needs and rights of children with regard to protection from torture and access to rehabilitation and redress. This is especially concerning given that torture tends to have even more severe and long-lasting effects on children than on adults, often leading to the interruption of the process of normal psychological, emotional and social development. Refugees and asylum seeker children may arrive traumatised and disorientated, separated from their families, forced by persecution to leave their own countries and come to the UK. Within the developmental process, the provision of care and healthy attachments in the early years is extremely important in helping refugee children and their carers while they are rebuilding their lives in the UK. Sadly, refugee families in Britain do not have equal access to the range of services and interventions available, even though the need for such a provision may be greater than in the general population as a whole. Knowing this from our experiences in therapeutic intervention and by the narratives that refugee and asylum seeker families tell us, we aim to address this inequality. We work to build the capacity of refugee community groups to enhance the ability of the carers to provide a better earlier service and to use the local authority provisions of such a service. It is known that asylum-seeking and refugee families often have multiple and complex social needs: poverty, benefit restrictions, a poor quality of temporary accommodation; and all of these have a major impact on children and their carers. Some asylum-seeking and refugee children, young people and their families may also have special healthcare needs, specifically psychological needs. Refugee children and young people, and in some cases their parents or carers, have particular linguistic barriers and do not speak English. The home language of communication for the child therefore remains in their first language. This may affect the child or young person's academic achievement. With more under-fives than in the general population, working with refugees and asylum seekers family with young children may have a greater need for intercultural approach dimension. Adult refugee parents with children in full time education are amongst the most unlikely people to go through the process of adaptation and settlement. They may also be suffering from psychological difficulties and not be able to cope. Many refugee mothers who usually have responsibility for the children have lost their informal support networks and their community they lived in, and that in itself can cause stress and psychological difficulties. Despite their great needs many asylum seeker and refugee families do not have access to the range of services that the general population does for complex and multiple reasons such as the lack of knowledge about services in this country. Many also move frequently because they are homeless or living in temporary accommodation, either in hostels or in other temporary accommodation. They may not want to place very young children with carers who do not speak the language the children speak at home, and are worried about possible racial harassment, which is quite a common feeling in refugees and therefore leads to an unwelcome feeling to the services provided in general. The local authorities do not usually have a clear inter-departmental planning and coordination for services for refugee and asylum seeker children and families. Refugee communities, groups or organisations also have very little resources to provide for young children, and as the refugee and asylum seeker families have multiple and social needs, expecting the national child care, child care agencies or services to provide or tailor the opportunity for refugee's needs could perhaps be too much to ask. Without a central policy being put into place, along with the presentation and dissemination of this central policy, the process of the integration of the family into society will be more difficult.

There is a wide gap between children of refugees' psychological needs and the services provided. Refugees' home countries, cultures, and social make-up are widely diversified, and their needs cannot be readily consolidated. This diversity of interest and need goes unacknowledged by the service-providers who may treat them as a single, homogenous group. Some refugees' needs are exaggerated, while others are ignored. This approach often ignores the justifiable and legitimate interest of refugees' psychological wellbeing. Many children of refugees may struggle with questions of race, ethnicity, language barriers, and other socio-political and economic issues that can influence their mental health and psychological wellbeing. Preoccupations of the child's emotions with those issues therefore have effects on child personality formations. These issues remain an inescapable subject for debate for establishment of appropriate services to meet the need of children and young people.

One may question if all of the legal issues related to refugees and asylum seekers can be useful for clinicians working with children of refugees and unaccompanied minors, indeed if they are relevant to the therapeutic intervention. The answer in my view is yes. In order to provide effective therapeutic intervention to children and young people, whether they are unaccompanied or with family, knowing the legal framework and human right issues are quite important. Apart from an overview of the relevant processes involved in therapeutic work and possible challenges therein, it is important for the therapist to have an overview of the child's situation in the past and any current issues. In the process of therapeutic intervention a therapist usually facilitates an environment for a child or an adolescent to look at both their day-to-day life here and now, as well as their past experiences.

From an intercultural perspective if the therapist works appropriately, the treatment can provide an understanding of the child's life. To do this successfully, the therapist needs to have a basic understanding of:

- Who unaccompanied children are;
- Asylum determination, lodging an application and the asylum process;
- The roles of different adults in the system;
- The legal and policy framework for support and care of the Children Act;
- The impact of the asylum process on care planning;
- Common issues faced by unaccompanied children and their carer.

CHAPTER ONE

What is torture?

Torture, whether physical or psychological depends on compli-cated interpersonal relationships or lack of relationships between the tortured person, the aggressive perpetrator (states and its officers ordering torture), the torturers and bystanders. Torture involves deeply personal processes in all those involved. These interacting psychological relationships, processes, and dynamics form the foundation and centre for the psychology of torture. Torture is about reprogram-ming the person to submit and surrender to a substitute interpretation of a specific situation, especially a religious one of the world, proffered by the states and its people in power abusing the position they hold. It is an act of, deep-seated, unforgettable, and traumatic indoctrination. There is always a question about applying diagnostic categories and descriptions of symptoms or behaviour developed in Western societies to people from the developing countries with very different personal, political, or religious beliefs and perspectives. One of the most manifest striking differences is between individualist societies where realisation of personal goals often takes priority over the needs of family, com-munity and societal expectations. In collectivist societies the needs of family and community stipulated roles take superiority over personal preferences. Another evident variance between Western and Eastern

1

societies is the belief in a subsequent life in which suffering in this life is rewarded after death. However, in Western society we note a different level of the psychological consequences of war, indeed the method of tackling radicalisations. One example is being on the side of state power like American veterans of the Vietnam War. This clearly could be understood as a political act which labelled the collective distress of a defeated and abused state as individual vulnerability and psychopathology in a distractive manner.

Protagonists of this and the de-politicisation of the distress of people who endured torture by describing their distress, disturbance, and profound sense of injustice in psychiatric terms, result in the development of the post-traumatic stress disorders. But, these are not only conceptual issues, it will affect the assessment and treatment of people who have endured torture and other forms of human rights violations, whether child or adult. The recovery of those affected therefore is associated with reconstruction of social and cultural systems and complexes, economic supports, and psychological respect for human rights.

Psychological consequences of torture

The creative and prolific research on treatment of PTSDs based on Vietnam veterans has substantially informed treatment offered to traumatised people and people affected by torture. It is more pertinent than the previous known treatments on behaviour therapy and medicalisations as the starting point from which to draw inferences or conclusions about unknown clinical presentations by veterans. The PTSD estimated a value that fell outside a range of already known values of psychiatric diagnostic criterial in the 1970s; i.e., those used to assess and diagnose civilian survivors of single events such as individual assault or accidents, or as communities or groups, such as natural or man-made disasters. Torture causes exceptional psychological problems that may decrease individual characteristics, often associated with particular issues and how the torturer aims to break the person as a whole physically, emotionally, and socially. Although the development of PTSD has provided useful clinical tools in legal terms, it is not an adequate description of the magnitude and complexity of the effects of torture, and is surely not useful for children who have endured torture. When the diagnosis of PTSD is applied, some people who endured torture with severe symptoms related to trauma may still not reach the criteria for diagnosis.

Categories such as complex trauma or adjustment disorder have been proposed as alternative diagnostic modified criteria. What is important to recognise is the fact that torture may cause profound and long lasting physical and psychological effects on the person who has endured torture. It is also important to recognise that torture does not just affect the person who has been tortured, but collectively may affect family members and friends. Those may include outbreaks of anger, withdrawal, depression or paranoia that affect the individual's manner when relating to family members and social interactions. Psychological and physical torture have similar mental effects and a person who experienced torture may suffer from elevated rates of anxiety, depression, adjustment, post-traumatic stress symptoms, and extreme stress not otherwise specified in diagnostic criterial, somatoform and occasionally psychotic manifestations, nightmares, intrusions, insomnia, decreased libido, memory lapses, reduced capacity to learn, sexual dysfunction, social withdrawal, emotional excitement or lack of excitement and monotonousness, periodic back pains and headaches. Both psychological and physical torture have similar mental effects and a person's presentation should be understood in the context of individual narratives, as diagnostic terminology cannot encapsulate the deep distrust of others which many people affected by torture have developed, nor the destruction of all that gave their lives meaning. For some the feelings of guilt, shame, and humiliation during the process of being tortured, and about the person's inability to withstand it, as well as potentially the guilt of surviving, can be causes of not trusting others and therefore the person is not able or willing to talk and disclose what actually happened. Above all of this suffering, there are concerns regarding immigration and other related matters, uncertainty about the future, including the possibility of being sent back to the country where the child or adult was tortured, and the lack of any close confidant or even of any social support. These multifarious stressors further add to the sense of social isolation, poverty, unemployment, homelessness, and substandard accommodation.

Rehabilitations

The aim of rehabilitation is to empower the person who endured torture to resume as full a life as possible. Rebuilding the life of someone whose dignity has been destroyed takes time and, as a result, long-term material, medical, psychological, and social support is needed.

Treatment must be a coordinated effort that covers both physical and psychological aspects. It is important to take into consideration the patients' needs, problems, expectations, views, and cultural references. The consequences of torture are likely to be influenced by many internal and external factors. Therefore, rehabilitation needs to employ different treatment approaches, taking into account the person's individual needs, as well as the cultural, social, and political environment. Rehabilitation centres around the world, notably the members of the International Rehabilitation Council for Torture Victims, commonly offer multi-disciplinary support and counselling, including:

- Medical attention/psychotherapeutic treatment;
- Psychosocial support/trauma treatment;
- Legal services and redress;
- Social reintegration.

In the case of asylum seekers and refugees, the services may also include assisting in documentation of torture for the asylum decision, language classes and help in finding somewhere to live and work.

In the worst case scenario, torture can affect several generations. The physical and mental after-effects of torture often place great strain on the entire family and society and particularly on children. In some cases, especially where torture was inflicted on children, the entire community can be traumatised where torture has been used in a systematic and widespread manner. In general, after years of repression, conflict, and war, the society's working structures have been broken or totally destroyed. Redress to address the practice of torture and trauma it causes can help reconstruct broken societies. Rehabilitation centres therefore play a key function for taking responsibility for advocating and disseminating democracy, co-existence and regard for and commitment to human rights. Rehabilitation services can provide support and hope, and act as a representation of attainment over the manufactured terror of torture which can hold back the development of democracy of entire societies.

CHAPTER TWO

Who is considered a refugee and an asylum seeker, and what are the procedures?

Refugees

A refugee is defined by the United Nations as:

> Any person who is outside their country of nationality and is unable to return due to a well-founded fear of persecution for reasons of race, religion, nationality, membership of a particular social group or political opinion.

The 1951 United Nations Convention Relating to the Status of Refugees has adopted the definition of a refugee (in Article 1.A.2) as any person who:

> Owing to a well-founded fear of being persecuted for reasons of race, religion, nationality, membership of a particular social group, or political opinion, is outside the country of his nationality, and is unable to or, owing to such fear, is unwilling to avail himself of the protection of that country.

The concept of a refugee was expanded by the Convention's 1967 Protocol and by regional conventions in Africa and Latin America to include persons who had fled war or other violence in their home country. The European Union's minimum standards definition of refugee, underlined by Article 2 (c) of Directive No. 2004/83/EC, essentially reproduces the narrow definition of a refugee offered by the UN 1951 Convention. Nevertheless, by virtue of articles 2 (e) and 15 of the same Directive, persons who have fled a war-caused generalised violence are, under certain conditions, eligible for a complementary form of protection, called subsidiary protection. The same form of protection is foreseen for people who, without being refugees, are nevertheless exposed, if returned to their countries of origin, to the death penalty, torture or other inhuman or degrading treatments. The term refugee is often used to include displaced persons who may fall outside the legal definition in the Convention, either because they have left their home countries due to war and not because of a fear of persecution, or because they have been forced to migrate within their home countries. The Convention Governing the Specific Aspects of Refugee Problems in Africa, adopted by the Organization of African Unity in 1969 (OAU, 1969), accepted the definition of the 1951 Refugee Convention and expanded it to include people who left their countries of origin not only because of persecution but also due to acts of external aggression, occupation, domination by foreign powers or serious disturbances of public order.

The lead international agency coordinating refugee protection is the Office of the United Nations High Commissioner for Refugees (UNHCR), which counted 8,400,000 refugees worldwide at the beginning of 2006. The major exception is the 4,600,000 Palestinian refugees under the authority of the United Nations Relief and Works Agency for Palestine Refugees in the Near East (UNRWA). In June 2011 the UNHCR estimated the number of refugees increased to 15.1 million. By and large the majority of refugees who leave their country seek asylum in the neighbouring countries. The robust needed solutions to refugee populations, as defined by UNHCR and governments, are voluntary repatriation to the country of origin, local integration into the country of asylum, and resettlement to a third country. One of the recent UNHCR's annual Global Trends Report states that:

> Worldwide displacement is at an all-time high and there is an expectation that it will increase even more. The number of people

forcibly displaced at the end of 2014 was 59.5 million, compared to 51.2 million a year earlier and 37.5 million a decade ago. One out of every 122 humans is now either a refugee, seeking asylum or internally displaced. If the number of displaced were compared to country populations, the displace population would be the world's 24th biggest country. Ongoing conflicts in Afghanistan and Somalia continue to create two of the largest groups of refugees, and the over the past five years, an additional 15 conflicts have erupted: eight in Africa (Burundi, Côte d'Ivoire, Central African Republic, Libya, Mali, north-eastern Nigeria, Democratic Republic of Congo, South Sudan); three in the Middle East (Syria, Iraq, and Yemen); one in Europe (Ukraine) and three in Asia (Kyrgyzstan, and in several areas of Myanmar and Pakistan). Syria is now the world's biggest producer of both internally displaced people (7.6 million) and refugees (3.88 million at the end of 2014). According to the Report, over half of all refugees are children. (UNHCR, World at War, 2015)

Asylum seekers

An asylum seeker is a person who has left their home country as a political refugee and is seeking asylum in another from fear of persecution for reasons of race, religion, social group, or political opinion, and has crossed an international border into a country in which he or she hopes to be granted refugee status. Asylum seekers have to recount details of past persecution to the immigration of nationality directorate in the host countries' Home Office. Following decisions made on individual cases, there can be three possible outcomes:

1. Full refugee status;
2. Exceptional leave to remain;
3. The case will be refused resulting in the removal and subsequently the deportation to the country of origin; the very one they desperately tried to escape from.

This definition reflects on the diversity of children's and young people's experiences, while taking into account each individual child's background, such as ethnicity, race, cultural identity, language, social and economic class, as well as what in legal terms constitutes a refugee.

The separation of these characteristics, although broad, does help to expand on the significant factors in an individual child's presentation which might be unfamiliar for an official. Further, it is important to recognise that in scrutinising the law, although the definition is often used to include refugee and asylum-seeking children aged under eighteen, it is by definition only related to adults.

The path and means of access to entitlements for asylum seekers in relation to key governmental and non-governmental structures, including an examination of the UK Border Agency that has been replaced by UK Visas and Immigration since 2013, are important for clinicians working with children of refugees and young people to know. This is for the reason that the asylum process is complex for patients and therefore might be challenging for therapists as well as other professionals new to the asylum field.

The 2013–2014 Seventh Report from the Home Affairs Committee proposed that asylum seekers, children, and victims of domestic violence or human trafficking should be exempt from the residence test for all civil proceedings. This is because, by virtue of their circumstances, they tend to be amongst the most vulnerable in society. The asylum seeker in the report is identified as a person seeking refuge from their country of origin and claiming rights described in paragraph 30 (1) of Part 1, Schedule 1, Legal Aid Sentencing and Punishment of Offenders Act 2012. This includes rights to enter and to remain in the United Kingdom arising from the Refugee Convention. In the government response to the seventh report from the home affairs committee session (2013–2014, HC 71), it stated that:

> The Legal Aid Agency (LAA) is committed to ensuring a good quality service. Quality is assured through various strands of work that we undertake with legal aid suppliers. The quality of processes is ensured through the requirement of all bidders for legal aid contracts to hold the relevant Specialist Quality Mark or the Lexel standard. The standards must be held prior to award of contract and throughout the lifetime of a contract [...]. We are not convinced that a separate support system for failed asylum seekers, whom the Government recognise as being unable to return to their country of origin, is necessary. The increasing period of time which asylum seekers have to wait for an initial decision suggests that staff resources could be better used by being allocated to asylum

applications. Section 4 is not the solution for people who have been refused but cannot be returned and we call on the Government to find a better way forward. We do not agree with the suggestion that failed asylum seekers should be treated, for the purposes of asylum support, in the same way as those who have yet to receive an initial decision. Failed asylum seekers can reasonably be expected to avoid the consequences of destitution by returning to their own countries. The Home Office meets the cost of the flight and provides generous reintegration assistance. Section 4 support is an appropriate safety net for the minority that encounter a temporary barrier to voluntary return, for example, because they need time to obtain the necessary travel documents from their national embassy. We make an exception for failed asylum seekers where there are children in the household. Section 95 support continues even if the claim is rejected in order to safeguard the welfare of the children. The Government does not believe that support should routinely continue in other cases. (2013, pp. 17–19)

The government response to the Seventh Report from the Home Affairs Committee session also indicated that the Independent Chief Inspector, in his 2013 description on unaccompanied asylum-seeking children, specifically checked for any evidence of a culture of disbelief amongst caseworkers who make age assessments in disputed minors' cases. He unmistakably rebutted the view that there is a culture of disbelief and speaks well of asylum staff for their cautious approach to age assessment and for giving the benefit of the doubt when appropriate stating:

Within this inspection, and contrary to the views held by some stakeholders, we did not find evidence of age dispute being a default position or of staff routinely disbelieving claims and failing to give the "benefit of the doubt". At all sites, we observed a focus on safeguarding with staff concerned to separate children from adults and get them promptly into Local Authority care. Several staff described their approach as treating each child as they would wish their own child to be treated if alone in a foreign country. (Paragraph 6.34)

The UK Border Agency (UKBA) was the border control agency of the British government and part of the Home Office that has been replaced by UK Visas and Immigration. It was formed as an executive agency on April 2008 by a merger of the Border and Immigration Agency (BIA), UK visas and the Detection functions of HM Revenue and Customs. The decision to create a single border control organisation was taken following a Cabinet Office report in which the agency came under proper criticism from the Parliamentary Ombudsman for consistently poor service, a backlog of hundreds of thousands of cases, and a large and increasing number of complaints. In the first nine months of 2009–2010, ninety-seven per cent of investigations reported by the Ombudsman resulted in a complaint against the agency being upheld. The complainants were asylum seeker residents, or other immigration applicants. On 26th March 2013, following a scathing report into the agency's ineffectiveness by the Home Affairs Select Committee, it was announced by Home Secretary Theresa May (UK Parliament, 2013) that the UK Border Agency would be abolished and its work returned to the Home Office. Its executive agency status was removed as of 31st March 2013 and the agency was split into two new organisations: UK Visas and Immigration focusing on the visa system, and Immigration Enforcement focusing on immigration law enforcement. The border control division of the UKBA had already been separated from the rest of the agency prior to this in April 2012 as the Border Force (BBC News, 26th March 2013).

Prior to July 2006, Home Office asylum support was administered by the National Asylum Support Service (NASS). NASS was established in 2000 as part of the former Immigration and Nationality Directorate within the Home Office and was responsible for organising the dispersal of asylum seekers away from London and the South-East of England to other areas of the UK. The package of support could involve enforced dispersal across the country. As part of the Home Office restructuring, NASS ceased to exist as a directorate in 2006 and at present all asylum support issues are dealt with and course of action are processed by New Asylum Model (NAM) caseworkers in the Home Office's newly formed Border and Immigration Agency (BIA).

Unaccompanied minor

According to the UN Declaration on the Rights of the Child, Comment 6, Section 7, unaccompanied asylum-seeking children in the United Kingdom, are children who are outside their country of origin to seek asylum in the United Kingdom; children who are separated from parents and relatives, and are not in the care of someone who is responsible for doing so. The United Nations describes unaccompanied children as: "Children, as defined in article 1 of the Convention, who have been separated from both parents and other relatives and are not being cared for by an adult who, by law or custom, is responsible for doing so." The United Nations defines separated children, a closely related group, as: "Children, as defined in article 1 of the Convention, who have been separated from both parents, or from their previous legal or customary primary caregiver, but not necessarily from other relatives. These may, therefore, include children being accompanied by adult family members." The UN Committee on the Rights of the Child, which the UK works to abide by, states that: "The appointment of a competent guardian as expeditiously as possible, serves a key procedural safeguard to ensure respect for the best interests of an unaccompanied or separated child."

The UK Home Office defines an unaccompanied asylum-seeking child as: "A person under 18, applying for asylum on his or her own right, who is separated from both parents and is not being cared for by an adult who by law has responsibility to do so." All asylum-seekers in the UK are seeking refugee status and the UK abides by the UN definition of a refugee when determining refugee status. The UN defines a refugee as a person who: "Owing to a well-founded fear of being persecuted for reasons of race, religion, nationality, membership of a particular social group or political opinion, is outside the country of his nationality and is unable or, owing to such fear, is unwilling to avail himself of the protection of that country."

The number of children unaccompanied arriving in the UK is increasing. Many are fleeing war, persecution, torture, poverty, drugs, and sexual violence in their home country or family home, but here in the United Kingdom, they're faced with a new set of challenges. Although there have been improvements, the system still is not equipped to handle the situation and therefore the future of refugee children and young people is filled with fears and uncertainty about the future while simultaneously dealing with past trauma. Children come unaccompanied to the UK for a variety of reasons. Some are escaping increasing violence and the lack of protection in their home communities, escaping stern austere abuse within the family; some are abandoned, or used for domestic and sexual exploitation, economic and social deprivation, forced marriage, prostitution, and female genital mutilation. Some are trafficked to the

UK for sexual and labour exploitation. Upon arrival, some children join family members they have never seen. In some cases these so called family members intention is motivated by using children and young people as slaves for domestic work and other factors. So, in addition to family separation these children are suffering in a very abusive home environment and are fearful to talk to anyone about what is happening to them. Their journeys may be as distressing as their experience in their home countries, potentially being subjected to sexual violence or other abuses as they travel. The children's challenges continue when they reach immigration authorities. The existing forms of immigration do not provide sufficient safeguards necessary to protect children under the Child Protection Act 1989.

There has been a growing recognition in the UK of the exceptional vulnerabilities and special needs of children in the immigration system, in particular unaccompanied children. Bearing witness to children's narratives in my work and by monitoring each child's situation, it is easy to identify that the major gaps in protection that remain in the immigration system for children are a lack of incorporation of the child protection principle, a lack of government appointed specialist advocacy support for children, and a lack of child-sensitive standards for the immigration process. The gravity of these gaps and the need to address them has become more and more apparent as the arrival of unaccompanied minors increases. The principles and standards of child protection should be considered as the foundation and the rule of law for protection of any child in the UK and internationally. In relation to children of refugees and unaccompanied minors, child welfare and juvenile justice systems should be required to follow all actions concerning the protection of children. Whether undertaken by public or private social welfare institutions, courts of law, administrative authorities or legislative bodies, child protection should act as a primary consideration. Failure to actively consider the child's protection can lead to children being sent back to countries where they have no dedicated adult to care for them or where their well-being, and even their life, is in danger, resulting in violations of children's human rights. Legal representation specialists need to be appointed for unaccompanied children in immigration proceedings. Further, children with limited education and, often, limited English skills, unconnected from adult care and detached from family and community connections, find it hard to understand or relate to the complex immigration procedures they face and the options and remedies that may be available to them under the law. Lacking appropriate adult care a child's experience during the immigration and welfare proceedings can be negative and in some cases traumatic.

The term unaccompanied minor usually refers to children less than eighteen years of age. The Home Office instruct their officers that where the age of the applicant and their status as a child is in doubt, reference should be made to the detailed guidance provided in the Asylum Instruction on Assessing Age, emphasising that the person whose age is in doubt should be treated as a child unless and until a full age assessment shows him or her to be an adult. The United Kingdom compared to many other countries has already taken significant steps towards improving protections for unaccompanied children and should be commended for these actions. Having said this, the reality shows that numbers of arriving children continue to grow, and highlights the need for further legal and policy reforms to ensure the rights and basic protections of these most vulnerable children who seek sanctuary in the UK are met. According to Home Office statistics (GOV.UK), between 2007 and 2011 there were on average 2,819 asylum applications from unaccompanied children each year. In 2011, there were a total of 1,277 applications from unaccompanied children.

The *Mail Online* reported that the:

> Number of unaccompanied child migrants being cared for by UK taxpayers has DOUBLED in the last three months and six more arrive here alone EVERY day. In the year to June, 2,168 under-18s entered Britain without their parents which is a rise of 46% over 2014 and latest figures show even faster increase. Kent County Council is now looking after 703 children, up from 369 in April, and the local authority's refuge site is over-capacity and over-budget (Joseph, 2015).

CHAPTER THREE

Care and protection of children

In recent years, one of the incidents that the UK public was horrified to learn of was the heart-breaking abduction of young April Jones. As this tragedy gripped national press networks, the protection of children has justifiably come to the forefront. Reflecting and comparing the two horrific acts of child abuse and neglect: the abduction of April Jones and the untimely death of Mrs G and her baby, it is shocking that the incident of Mrs G and her baby failed to take hold of national attention in the same way the abduction of April Jones quite rightly did. It is only when one can consider the media's portrayal of these two unbearable calamities that we are able to distinguish a readily overlooked subliminal discourse of race and social class unfolding, dismissive of egregious and flagrant violations of the human rights of refugee and asylum-seeking communities. Human rights are not just for some, all humans have an inalienable entitlement to all rights regardless of race, culture, class, ethnicity, sexuality, ability, and economic power. Many young asylum seekers and refugee families face multiple social problems including difficulties making an asylum application, finding a proper solicitor, living in poor housing, poverty, difficulty accessing and receiving benefits, and lack of knowledge about services. Some parents we serve feel that their social difficulties are preventing them from being good parents.

Specifically depression amongst mothers, caused by social distress and isolation, increases the worry for their children as they are aware that they are not being emotionally there for their children, or their stress causes them to be emotionally absent. In their therapy many asylum seekers express a deep feeling of sadness and isolation, acutely feeling the loss of support networks from their families or extended families, and being isolated due to lack of English language skills, and in some cases a fear of going out in some parts of London or outside London because of the racial harassment and lack of contact with their community. These isolated mothers feel very uncomfortable leaving their young children at child minders or in a nursery from outside their community, especially in a community where no one speaks their home language. The majority of parents we see at the Refugee Therapy Centre are usually unaware of the low cost or free services for young children, such as libraries or toy libraries, or play groups or play sessions in the community centres, sport centres or schools, they are not even aware of the after school clubs or homework clubs for older children at school. All of this highlights the lack of early psycho-social intervention or provision and dissemination of information for asylum-seeking young families, especially where they may have direct experience of racial harassment in the form of being bullied at school or when they change schools or the neighbourhood they live in. Some parents who reported not being able to cope or being violent physically or verbally are quite worried about their parenting skills and that is why they ask for help from us. They are also extremely worried about how social workers and social services perceive their parenting skills. Some parents also expressed worry about teachers because they are aware of the cultural differences of childhood, specifically their understanding of physical punishment as an acceptable form of discipline which may not be shared by a teacher. They are very concerned when child protection issues are raised with them and it is proposed that they get help and a proper assessment. They express a great fear that social workers will accuse them of physical abuse or neglect and take their children away, and they need great support and encouragement to be able to use resources from social services available to them when they are not able to cope. One common fear amongst almost all different cultural backgrounds is separation from their children and lack of trust. Some asylum-seeking families are able to use and get in touch with the refugee community organisations, but they may not live close enough to these organisations to get support and some asylum seekers and refugees do not wish to contact refugee community organisations they do not know personally and they can't trust. Some female clients also indicate that community organisations can be very much male dominated and it is quite unlikely they would get involved in the woman's needs or issues, such as child care or a woman's wish to improve her language. This is especially the case in some communities such as Somalian, Eritrean, and Kurdish communities. Psychological intervention can play an important role in meeting the needs of children and families of refugees and asylum seekers. Combating social exclusion and preventing further stress results in healthy development for children of refugees and further decreases youngsters acting out their aggression in the community, or seeking to join radical groups. Some parents sometimes express concern that their children lose their language and culture of their home country. They are concerned that their children will grow up with very different values to their own and their families and become alienated from their parents as a result. There is a reality that supports this fear as the younger generation of children learn English very quickly in comparison to their parents. This can create a fear in the parents of the children losing the old culture. On the other hand it is also likely that the parents will use their young children as interpreters and translators without recognising that the level of understanding that their child has of the English Language is still only at the level that the child has reached developmentally in their own language and culture. The child's level is not an adult level of language and that in itself can create further trauma to children and young people. As discussed before, with more under-fives than in the general population, and also young children over five and adolescents, refugees and asylum seekers families, especially some of the newcomers, may have a greater need for earlier provision of service. This in itself indicates that it is not good practice to put refugee children in an equal position to the general or indigenous population. The lack of training and courses on refugee's issues, language, working with interpreters, and anti-discriminatory practice, prevents professionals from meeting the refugee children's healthcare and emotional needs and it prevents these children and families from using the healthcare professionals within the community during the early years. Taking care of and protecting the welfare and rights of children should be the primary concern of all professionals involved in the care of children, including staff working within the UK Border Agency and local authorities. Although discussion in this book focuses on refugee children, the principles and practices described apply to all migrant children. The UK Border Agency frequently has poor and inconsistent decision-making in regards to children. Children and their carers report that in their experiences the officials are harsh and insensitive towards refugee children. Having said that, this book's aim is not to criticise any agency, but is intended to look at issues in a constructive and informative method, to share techniques and tactics to challenge the deficiencies in the UK asylum process, and aid those involved in the protection of the welfare of children to consider their practices to see how they can be improved and developed in order to ensure that they play their part.

The protection of refugee children in the UK and the introduction of Section 55 of the Borders, Citizenship and Immigration Act 2009 places an obligation on all public and private welfare institutions, courts of law, administrative authorities, and legislative bodies to "safeguard and promote the welfare of children who are in the United Kingdom". It indicates that: "The Secretary of State must make arrangements for ensuring that functions are discharged having regard to the need to safeguard and promote the welfare of children who are in the United Kingdom [...]." Section 55 is principally linked with the entitlements also maintained in the United Nations Convention on the Rights of the Child which, in Article 12, emphasises the importance of children being heard and being provided with the opportunity to express their own views in matters concerning them. This is recognised as "the voice of the child" which has sustained the importance of the reservation to the Convention which the UK also supported in relation to children subject to immigration control. The adoption of the Convention and the introduction of section 55 into the UK law have an impact on the rights of the children. The connection between the Convention and Section 55 is presented with clarity in the accompanying Statutory Guidance issued to the UK Border Agency which makes it clear that children have the right to be consulted and express views on matters concerning them. The Statutory Guidance confirms the public duty to listen to and hear the child. It is about providing children with high quality representation to ensure that children's voices and concerns are well and truly hear.

Asylum procedures and mental health

Children's mental health and development should be central to making decisions about their asylum application. This means making sure that they are healthy, have an allocated social worker and guardian, somewhere safe to live, access to legal support appropriate to their age and need, appropriate support enabling them to achieve in education, and be entitled to and encouraged to access out of school activities to ease the process of integration, assimilation and acculturalisation. Based on the narratives of the children and young people we provide services for, we are concerned about disparity in services for children in different boroughs and different regions in the UK. The fact that the lives of children who are separated from their families for reasons beyond their control is a reality that needs to be taken into consideration in every step of care and by all services. Many unaccompanied children or even those living with family sometimes don't have a trusted adult looking after them. Another serious concern is the level of destitution facing refugee and asylum-seeking children. On a daily basis we hear from such children how they feel unwanted, rejected and are treated badly. They feel they are not human and no one cares. The children that experience destitution are a demonstration and confirmation that incredibly vulnerable young people are being left destitute, hungry and in danger. They are compelled to resort to progressively more desperate and dangerous means to survive physically.

In their report in 2012 the Refugee Council indicated that many asylum-seeking women who are destitute are vulnerable to violence in the UK and more than twenty per cent of the women accessing their services had experienced sexual violence in the UK. (Refugee Council, 2012).

The Government has reduced the asylum support for children, which was already alarmingly low. This means children and young people have had a cut of thirty per cent in their welfare income, while the cost of food is increasing. Monitoring and analysing the data of my work indicates that children are growing up in households without proper food, heating or any love and support. I hear that mothers feel forced to prostitute themselves in order to survive, and that some refused asylum seekers or destitute pregnant women cannot afford to eat or access vital health care.

Another matter related to children and young people is child trafficking, child pornography, and the trafficking of children for sexual purposes. Children exposed to trafficking need additional support and protection to help them escape exploitative, manipulative, and abusive situations. Often, when we are taking the child and young person narratives into accounts, we identify that children involved in illegal activities due to coercion are treated as criminals rather than recognised as vulnerable victims who need support and supervisions, as well as specialist therapeutic support to help them to break the cycle of violence and to move forward in their lives in a positive way.

The UK Children Society reported that more than 3,000 children arrive in the UK alone every year seeking asylum. The "Our going it alone" children in the asylum process report, published in 2007, highlights the barriers and unequal treatment children face as they struggle to navigate complex and adult systems to get the support they need. This policy briefing describes the asylum process from the perspective of the unaccompanied children, and is based on extensive consultation with the young people.

Currently, children as young as twelve are interviewed about the substance of their asylum application. Discretion is also allowed to be used on whether to interview in cases where the child is younger and considered to be mature and, if given the option, is willing to be interviewed. Physical and mental health considerations need to be taken into account when considering whether going ahead with an interview is in the child's best interests. Although is not practised regularly, case workers could, in consultation with the social worker, accompanying adult or other responsible adult, and the legal representative, select a suitable location for the substantive interview.

Life after gaining refugee status

Those with refugee status have full entitlement to welfare benefits, housing and health care and employment. However, there has been a shift to more temporary protection rather than indefinite leave to remain. Refugees now have their cases reviewed after five years, and those with Humanitarian Protection or Discretionary Leave are normally reviewed earlier than that. So there is a need to have some level of knowledge about the immigration issues and a specific understanding of the needs of refugee pupils, including those new to schooling in the UK. This helps to look into exploring the existential issues and consider positive strategies to support children and young people in achieving their potential. We need to reflect on and evaluate our own practice, as well as that of the school systems that service these children. To better inform our practice and all services that support children of refugees, young people and their families we need to stay aware of:

- The refugee psychological, cultural, and social experiences;
- The needs of children, focusing on the immediate and longer term needs;
- Supporting children who have endured or who were exposed to torture and human rights violations;
- To ensure the school ethos and learning environment promote inclusion;
- Ensuring the specific needs of refugee pupils are met in a timely manner;
- Learning and teaching—strategies that support resilience and achievement.

Here I will bring an example of how people's lives can be lost within the system partly due to lack of English language, lack of knowledge, lack of appropriate services that can take language and other cultural elements into accounts, indeed, the lack of clarity about policies on the part of professionals. Mrs G and her baby boy, who I have briefly mentioned before, sought asylum in the UK and successfully gained refugee status. However, even after she gained her status, she and her baby boy slipped through the cracks of state support and tragically died of causes related to homelessness and hunger. This was a shocking incident that happened in the heart of London, Westminster. We might ask why this has happened in the twenty-first century, but it has happened and it is important to learn some lessons for future prevention of such occurrences. When policies designed to ostensibly lessen deprivation for vulnerable people result in imposed destitution, critical reflection becomes glaringly unavoidable. This reflection, however necessary, has arrived too late for Mrs G and her baby boy, who tragically lost their lives to a failed system of State support, media negligence and a fundamental denial of their human rights. On 5th October 2012, Amelia Gentleman's article in *The Guardian* titled: "Double death in asylum seeker family reveals gap in state benefits", quoted Dave Garratt, the chief executive of Refugee Action, as saying:

> The transition from NASS support to full state benefit entitlement funded by the Department for Work and Pensions continues to fail

some of the most vulnerable and marginalised people in society. Unacceptable delays in these transition arrangements are all too common, resulting in homelessness and hunger.

Despite serious warnings in the case review following the preventable death of this asylum-seeking mother and child, the response from the Home Office has been to increasingly unravel what minimal support the State provided asylum seekers in transition through support schemes. In the absence of such services, the government assured those concerned that support would be available through the voluntary sector, in a largely unrestrained repositioning of responsibility. As the current economic recession has highlighted through socio-political debate, such government tactics of dissociating from and offloading accountability onto the third sector for the assurance of basic human rights is becoming increasingly frequent.

Responding to those children and young people who fled torture and persecution in search of refuge with policies of forced destitution is, at worst, an extreme violation of basic human rights and, at best, a bureaucratic failure. Looking beyond the brief and passing headlines, a shameful picture emerges of a system bound by racialist and total exclusion from mainstream society and its advantages. Politicians are not addressing issues of social exclusion that lay claim to a hierarchy of human worth based on class structure and social order with a focus on capital. This structural social inequality, and consequent lack of social responsibility, indignantly undermines the UK domestic Human Rights law as well as international conventions such as the 1948 Universal Declaration of Human Rights to which the UK Government is a signatory.

CHAPTER FOUR

Human rights

The foundations of the human rights obligation to prohibit and eliminate all corporal and all other degrading forms of punishment, lie in the rights of every person to respect for his or her dignity and physical integrity, and to equal protection under the law. The original International Bill of Human Rights adopted and proclaimed by General Assembly resolution 217 A (III) in the 10th December 1948 states that: "The dignity of each and every individual is the fundamental guiding principle of international human rights law", (paragraph 16) and shows how the Convention on the Rights of the Child builds on these principles. Article 19 of the Convention, requires States to protect children "from all forms of physical or mental violence." This is helpful although it is limited as the term "all forms of physical or mental violence" does not safeguard or ensure a total protection for so many vulnerable children, and leaves room for some level of legalised violence against children. Corporal punishment, torture, child soldiers and other cruel or degrading forms of punishment are forms of violence and the State must take responsibility and implement appropriate and seemly legislative, administrative, social, and educational measures to eliminate any violence towards children. Abolishing and eradicating violations against children, through implementation of law and other social

23

and political measures, is an immediate responsibility and obligation of all nations states.

It is clear that the practice of violence directly conflicts with the equal and unchallengeable right of children to respect for their human dignity and physical integrity. The distinct nature of children, their initial dependence in the process of development, their unique human potential, their resiliency as well as their vulnerability, all require the need for more, rather than a lesser amount of legal and other forms of care and protection from all forms of violence.

Along with other concerned members of society, I feel compelled to raise the question of what could have happened differently to prevent such a senseless and tragic way of life for children and young people who experienced torture directly or were exposed to torture by witnessing their loved one being tortured. Although children's vulnerability to torture is well known, there are not right and proper provisions for support and rehabilitations as it should be. After arrival in the country where they are seeking asylum, no psychological or therapeutic help is provided to people. There are indeed many more people in the host countries who are in similar positions and whose psychological needs are not being attended to, potentially rendering catastrophic circumstances in the general population. While the lack of, or incoherence of material support may be a primary factor, the absence of systemic support services is a concern. If the relevant support system could be made available, there will be a greater potential for filling the gaps that ultimately affect refugee children and young people who have endured and been exposed to torture. As individuals, it is our duty to collectively defend human rights, which is not merely about providing material support to those in need, but also about helping those within society to gain the psychological and emotional resilience to become self-sufficient and positive and contributing members of their new society. The diversity of factors embodied in children of refugee and asylum seeker experiences are often cause for extreme vulnerability; thus, our neglect of the psychological needs of these communities is just as dire as the absence of any other support services.

As a society firmly committed to human rights, in the UK and abroad, we are obliged to recognise the vital need for appropriate interventions particularly for the most vulnerable in society. To pay lip service to this recognition, however, is not enough; explicit support and acknowledgement from government and decision makers of this basic right is crucial. Until appropriate support is made available and easily accessible for all those children and young people who are in need, and not merely those able to pay or those who are acclimatised to British cultural norms, our duty, and indeed the state duty, to serve human rights remains unfulfilled.

To place the blame for tragedy that children have endured disproportionately upon the apparatuses of the UK or other States where tortured children seek refuge would be misguided. The media has long maintained a deafening silence to the injustices endured by the refugee and asylum-seeking children and adults, and the tragedies suffered in those communities that they are coming from, bringing only punitive and dehumanising accounts to the public eye.

Gentleman's (5th October 2012) solitary reporting to *The Guardian*, previously mentioned, informed the nation of the horrifying situation in which Mrs G and her baby's lives were unnecessarily lost, revealing not only failures of the asylum system, but also the prejudice within society at large as no other journalists had found it relevant and noteworthy to cover. This means we are living in a society that has reached a deeply concerning moment when mainstream media predominantly demands our attention for the trivial, and when reporting on the critical issues affecting human lives, routinely omits the experiences of the socially and economically excluded except when to confirm well-rehearsed stereotypes. This alarming death of this mother and child should be a lesson for state, public and voluntary services to find a way to close the gaps in the services necessary for protection of children and vulnerable adults.

We regularly bear witness to narratives of refugee and asylum seeker children and young people who are experiencing discrimination in their daily lives and therefore feel they are more likely to experience poor treatment. Increasing accessibility of appropriate support is one channel that should not be underestimated by government and service providers. So, it is fundamental for our work to have knowledge and respect of human rights and right of children in every step we are taking in providing services to refugee children and young people. We need to set a method ensuing the outcome of services we are providing is based on human right and guarantee accountability within our social and political institutions.

We should aspire to create a world where all children and young people are respected, valued and heard. In our efforts towards this end, we specifically should focus our attentions and resources on children of refugees and their families. Our collective thinking and action and our general objectives should include our conviction that childhood should be happy for all children in the world regardless of their ethnicity, race, class, colour, and cultural outlook; that all young people deserve to reach their full potential; and that refugee children should be provided the support they need to become good members of society. Day after day we need to have commitment to these objectives and to work to transform the lives of children of refugees, young people and their families in the UK and other countries in which children seek refuge.

In provision of care for children of refugees we should address internal emotional distress, as well as the external, practical problems which cause it, particularly looking at:

• The main causes of distress and disturbance in children, including trauma, effect of torture or other forms of human right violations and losses;
• The differences and similarities between distress and mental illness;
• The distinction between different models of intervention based on the individual child's experiences and the needs;
• All-inclusive assessment of needs;
• The principles of risk assessment in terms of individual child;
• Constantly seeking to employ interventions that respect differences;
• To move away from western interventions at an individual level and to run projects based on feedback received from the service users;
• Focus on social reconstruction, social reconciliation and healing;
• Work with families and communities in an effort to restore social structures and a sense of routine and normality;
• Not lead by stereotypical notions of social norms, values, dynamics and power; structures; instead, focus on the need to contextualise projects and give greater attention to ethnographic needs.

Reorienting our approach in this way, we can assure greater resilience, sustainability, and closer social and cultural adaptation for children and young people in the new community. Such an approach at times can be criticised as being imprecise and lacking a firm, quantified data. This criticism mostly comes from people or services that do not have knowledge or understanding of the needs of children who have experienced torture and thus hold inaccurate views. Contrary to this, the arguing in favour of the perspective that children are resourceful is not to sanction their exposure to adversity, nor to deny that some children may be rendered very vulnerable who need to be attended too in a timely manner. It is important to question normative ideas about childhood weakness and consider whether a focus on children's vulnerabilities is really the most effective way of supporting self-esteem and self-efficacy in adverse environments. The practical value of an understanding of children as resourceful is that it builds on children's strengths, rather than emphasising their ill-health, vulnerability, weakness, and dependency.

Ensuring the well-being of unaccompanied children and young people who have endured torture and violence should be at the heart of services. Suitable information and tools are needed to ensure appropriate processes are in place within the society to serve children in the best possible way. We need to strive to build our practical understanding of the impact of cultural background on the age assessment process and the legislative and policy framework of Children's Services and the UK Visas and Immigration. Using this knowledge, we should consider the impact of gender-based violence in a systemic context, looking at potential consequences it may have on the lives of asylum-seeking girls and young women according to their varied experiences in the country of origin, and indeed in the host country. Examining the effects of gender-based violence from individual, family and community perspectives presents the opportunity to explore practical ways of overcoming barriers to accessing health and other services, bearing in mind an overview of child protection legislation, issues affecting children and families from abroad, as well as identification and referral processes available with this country.

Torturing children and human rights

The perpetration of torture is a complex issue. It is important to recognise that the legal, the social, and psychological dimensions of torture are interlinked. The practical and abstract legal considerations are interwoven with socio-psychological factors. These elements need to be addressed to contextualise the dynamics of torture that impact those children and young people subjected to torture. It is important to look at the legal issues specifically in line with Article 1 of the Human Rights Convention. Therefore, there is a need to focus on the perpetration of torture as a complex issue and to look at evidence that exists regarding children in countries in which torture is currently practiced in the context of torture as a worldwide problem. There is a need to address these complex elements and contextualise the dynamics of human rights. There are as yet no official or reliable independent statistics for measuring the scale of the problem.

The definition of the Convention against Torture and Other Cruel, Inhuman or Degrading Treatment or Punishment applies to children as well as adults. The Convention was adopted and opened for signature, ratification, and accession by General Assembly resolution 39/46 of 10th December 1984 and entered into force on 26th June 1987, in accordance with Article 27 (1). The State Parties to this Convention recognise that, in accordance with the principles proclaimed in the Charter of the United Nations (1945), recognition of the equal and inalienable rights of all members of the human family is the foundation of freedom, justice and peace in the world, recognising that those rights derive from the inherent dignity of the human person. States are obligated under the Charter, in particular Article 55, to promote universal respect for, and observance of, human rights and fundamental freedoms, and to have regard for Article 5 of the Universal Declaration of Human Rights and article 7 of the International Covenant on Civil and Political Rights, both of which provide that no one shall be subjected to torture or to cruel, inhuman or degrading treatment or punishment. This is in line with the Declaration on the Protection of All Persons from Being Subjected to Torture and Other Cruel, Inhuman or Degrading Treatment or Punishment, adopted by the General Assembly on 9th December 1975. Children are tortured during political violence and war conflicts in many countries around the world. It was not long ago that Nazi persecution, arrests, and deportations were directed against all members of Jewish and Gypsy families, regardless of age, gender, or class. There were homeless and often orphaned children, many of whom had witnessed the murder of their parents, siblings, and relatives, and who were facing starvation, illness, brutal labour, and other terrors before they were consigned to the gas chambers. Over a million children under the age of sixteen died in the Holocaust. Taken from their homes and stripped of their childhood they lived and died during the dark years of the Nazi Holocaust.

Lucie Adelsberger, (1885–1971) a Jewish female physician, describes in her memoir the horror she experienced in Auschwitz while working in the sanatorium of the notorious death camp's Gypsy section, and the ordeals suffered by so many vulnerable in the camps. Her account operates as a disturbing reminder of the horrors perpetrated by the Nazi. Throughout her memoir, Adelsberger portrays the methods the Nazis used to humiliate, demean and dehumanise Jews and other Holocaust sufferers, stripping them of their dignity, their freedom, and more often than not, their lives. Adelsberger's (2003) testament to the human suffering at Auschwitz describes the life of the children and said, like the adults, the children were only a mere bag of bones, without muscles or fat, and the thin skin erased through and through beyond the hard bones of the skeleton and ignited itself to ulcerated wounds. Blisters and eruptions covered the underfed body from the top to the bottom and thus deprived it of energy.

Before the Holocaust, a significant portion of Armenian children perished due to human rights violations during the Armenian Genocide. Talaat, the Minister of the Interior of the Ottoman Empire at the time said:

"All the Armenians in the country who are Ottoman subjects, from five years of age upwards, are to be taken out of the towns and slaughtered". Some children were burnt alive; the others were poisoned or drowned, some died from lack of food or diseases and hundreds of thousands of Armenian children were left orphans, and only children of those who were forced to convert to Islam to survive steady alive. One of the most extensive operations of mass burning of children took place in Bitlis province. Swedish missionary Alma Johansson, who was running the German orphanage in Mush, reported that many Armenian women and children were burnt alive and the orphans burned in their orphanage. The mass burning of children took place also in Der Zor, where the orphans were gathered into a large orphanage building, then were pushed in batches to a spot about an hour distant from the city, doused with petrol and torched to death. This method of murder of children was implemented also in the provinces of Kharpert and Diyarbakir. The method of poisoning of children was also implemented by Turkish physicians during these years. Survivors testify how in Ageon, Khapert province, Armenian orphans collected from all parts of the province were poisoned through arrangements with the local pharmacist and physician. Nearly all methods of genocide were implemented at Trabzon. Dr Ziya Fuad, Inspector of Health Services, and Dr Adnan, the city's Health Services Director, testified based on evidence gathered from local Turkish physicians that Dr Ali Saib, Director of Public Health of Trabzon province, systematically poisoned Armenian infants brought to the city's Red Crescent Hospital and ordered the drowning at the nearby Black Sea of those who resisted taking his "medicine". Another method Dr Saib applied in a house full of Armenian infants was the "steam bath".

A large number of Armenian children were killed through mass drowning at the Mesopotamian lower ends of the Euphrates River, especially in the area of Deir Zor. According to the testimony of an Armenian survivor, on October 24th 1916 Deir Zor's police chief ordered some 2,000 Armenian orphans to be carried to the banks of the Euphrates. Their hands and feet bound, the children were thrown into the river two by two to the visible enjoyment of the police chief Mustafa Sidki, who took special pleasure at the sight of the children drowning. Another centre for mass murder of children through drowning was the Kemakh Gorge on the Euphrates River. The US Ambassador, Henry Morgenthau, states that at Kemakh Gorge: "Hundreds of children were bayoneted by the Turks and thrown into the Euphrates". The policy of the Turkish Government to annihilate the Armenian children became more evident after the deportation, when a lot of orphans were gathered. The Turkish Government opened orphanages for these children. Talaat, the Minister of the Interior, was ordered to collect and keep only those orphans who could not remember the tortures to which their parents had been subjected. The others should be sent away with caravans. Danish missionary, Sister Hansina Marcher, visited one of these orphanages in Kharpert and found about 700 Armenian children; all of them were well clothed and fed. When she visited the orphanage again several days later, there were only 13 out of the 700 children left. The rest had disappeared. They had been taken to a lake and drowned, where tens of thousands of Armenians were drowned during that summer (Akçam, 2013; Alayarian, 2008).

Taner Akçam in his book, *The Young Turks' Crime against Humanity: The Armenian Genocide and Ethnic Cleansing in the Ottoman Empire*, (2013) introduced new evidence from more than 600 secret Ottoman documents. He demonstrated in detail that the Armenian Genocide and the expulsion of Greeks from the late Ottoman Empire resulted from an official effort to get rid the Christians. Presenting these previously inaccessible documents, along with expert context and analysis, Akçam's work goes deep inside the bureaucratic machinery of Ottoman Turkey and shows how a dying empire embraced genocide and ethnic cleansing. Although the deportation and killing of Armenians was internationally condemned in 1915 as a "crime against humanity and civilization", the Ottoman government initiated a policy of denial that is still maintained by the Turkish Republic. A century after the Armenian genocide and many decades of holocaust, the children at high-risk of torture today usually are those impoverished living in the street, deprived of parental care, in conflict with the law, in detention and, indeed, children whose parents are politically active in opposition to oppressive regimes. During political violence and war the high-risk children are the children detained during aggression fighting and warfare, children are used as soldiers. Children of internally displaced, those living in temporary camps, and children of refugees are amongst the most vulnerable. It is important to look at the legal issues specifically in line with Article 1 of the Convention, which defines torture as:

> Any act by which severe pain or suffering, whether physical or mental, is intentionally inflicted on a person for such purposes as obtaining from him or a third person, information or a confession, punishing him for an act he or a third person has committed or is suspected of having committed, or intimidating or coercing him or a third person, or for any reason based on discrimination of any kind, when such pain or suffering is inflicted by or at the instigation of or with the consent or acquiescence of a public official or other person acting in an official capacity. It does not include pain or suffering arising only from, inherent in or incidental to lawful sanctions.

Convention Against Torture (1984), Article 1.1. This is in line with Article 2 of the Convention that prohibits torture, and requires parties to take effective measures to prevent it in any territory under its jurisdiction. This prohibition is absolute. No exceptional circumstances may be invoked and called upon to justify torture, including war, threat of war, internal political instability, public emergency, terrorist acts, violent crime, or any other form of armed conflict.

Amnesty International (2007) reported that child torture remains widespread in the world. The countries carrying out torture on children include Afghanistan, Algeria, Angola, Brazil, Burundi, China, Colombia, Democratic Republic of Congo, Ecuador, Eritrea, Ethiopia, Lebanon, Georgia, Mexico, Nepal, Honduras, Mongolia, Moldova, Israel occupied territories, Iraq, Iran, Paraguay, Serbia, Sudan, Saudi Arabia, Sri Lanka, South Africa, Swaziland, and many other places. So, looking into the future, there is a great need to act in order to put a stop to this and save children from torture. It goes without saying that there is an immediate need to intervene on behalf of the children exposed to torture in the realm of policy and legal accountability. Indeed there is an urgent need to provide solutions and pathways to well-being after violations have occurred. It is our role as clinicians and as frontline people involved in the care of vulnerable children to take the lead for helping children who have endured torture and other violations, and to work simultaneously with other professionals and campaigners towards prevention and provision of appropriate rehabilitation and care in response to this dangerous and precarious subject matter.

The largest group of tortured children today is amongst refugees. There are high numbers of unaccompanied children, mainly from Latin America, Africa, and the Middle-east, who arrive in foreign lands after fleeing profound and unfathomable forms of violence and oppression. Within this diverse demographic also are child soldiers, children affected by armed conflict and street violence, also those tortured as a result of extreme poverty, and others abandoned or subjected to child labour and slavery.

Apart from direct torture of children, in the context of wider human rights violations, there are also indirect traumatic experiences, used as emotional torture of children. These include:

- Political killing of a child's primary carer or their loved one;
- Deliberate use of lethal force against a child, parents of the child, family members or group in the community by an agency serving state or such a power;
- Illegal and disproportionate use of lethal force against a child, parents of the child, family members or group in the community by an agency serving state or such a power;
- In armed conflicts, the disproportionate use of force, an attack against a child, parents of the child, family members or group in the community by an agency serving state or such a power;

- Failure of the state to prevent loss of life by failing to act in situations where there is a clear threat to the child's life or against a child, parents of the child, family members or group in the community.

Children, who are maltreated and persecuted by torture and war, and indeed other forms of human rights violations, are often perceived only in terms of vulnerability. It is also important to mention that the trafficking of children continues to be a major international problem that has been rapidly increasing into the twenty-first century. This book discusses the problems with such a perspective and its implications on effective boundaries and treatment focussing on the devastating consequences of children and young people who are subjected to such abuse.

Looking at international activities supporting the prosecution of perpetrators of torture and other human rights violations, and specifically drawing on the work of International Rehabilitation Council for Torture Victims, this discussion aims to look at the effectiveness of international conventions on the accountability of perpetrators, making suggestions for further work. It is helpful for children subjected to torture if professionals coordinate their efforts at the international, regional, and local levels as such as realistically as possible. How we intervene as professionals with children of refugees and unaccompanied minors has a lasting effect on that child's well-being and future capacity as an adult to cope with challenges in life. The process of "dissociation" and resilience-focused treatment, based on the work of the Refugee Therapy Centre where a substantive portion of resilience research and development has occurred, are considered appropriate clinical interventions for children who have endured torture directly or indirectly, or who have been exposed to other forms of trauma.

Specifically drawing on the work of International Rehabilitation Council for Torture Victims is helpful to identify the effectiveness of international conventions on the accountability of perpetrators. Interactions and dissemination of knowledge between professionals working with children of refugees and unaccompanied minors who have been tortured, is valuable ways of providing appropriate rehabilitation service. The subject for debates is to clearly identify how torture can have a lasting effect on that child's wellbeing and capacity to cope with challenges in life in an adult life. Discussions and knowledge sharing between professionals is way forwards for the best practice. Discussion on the positive use of healthy dissociations (2011) based on my work at the work of the Refugee Therapy Centre together with a substantive portion of resilience research and developments can help identification of the psychological issues arisen from torture and the doctrine of resilience-focused therapeutic intervention for treatments of children should be combined with the legal and socio-psychological dimensions of helping children and young people who have endured torture.

A lesson from the case of Manisa

I will bring in an example here.

On 26th of December 1995, sixteen students from Manisa, Turkey were arrested for subversive activities, such as displaying left-wing posters and causing a fire in a barber shop. The youngest of those arrested was fourteen years old, the oldest in his early twenties. Most were between fifteen and eighteen. The teens were detained for nine days before being allowed to see their parents. The students were originally convicted of belonging to an illegal leftist group, the Revolutionary People's Liberation Front in 1997, and were acquitted in 2000. They were tortured into a coerced confession, and some even had to be sent to the hospital while still in custody to be treated for the abuse they received out of sight at the hands of the police. The students reported the use of electric shock, as well as pressurised water to hose down the detainees to persuade and coax a confession. The boys reported that they were forced to strip naked while officers squeezed and twisted their genitals. They claimed to have been anally raped with batons and truncheons. The females underwent forced vaginal exams, and one was reportedly raped.

The case was taken to court and the medical evidence proving the guilt of the officers was so strong that the Court of Appeals twice overturned lower courts decisions to acquit the officers. Finally, in 2002, the police officers were convicted and sentenced to serve between five and twelve years each. The Court of Appeals upheld the conviction of the ten officers in April of 2003.

Much public pressure fell on the Turkish government to uphold their pledge to take action against torture. The European Union demanded reform in Turkey's human rights policies before the country would be allowed entrance into the European Union. According to Sabir Ergul of the Republican People's Party, the original acquittals of the officers would make "Turkey hang its head in shame before the civilized world". Amnesty International hailed the sentencing of the officers as a "positive step in the fight against impunity for torture in Turkey".

The right to freedom of expression and the right to peaceful protest are central in a democracy and transparency in Government and help to inform political debate. Based on these basic principles no one shall be subjected to torture or to inhuman or degrading treatment or punishment for expressing views or organise and or join protest. Governments developing security should not influence or limits dialogues, communications, and discourses. Such limitation in society leads to moral indifference and a narrow-minded intolerant approach in the name of security is an oppressive contented self-righteous rule that is in contrast to human rights and international humanitarian concerns.

Human rights are an unchallengeable, incontrovertible, and indisputable right that cannot be taken away for any reason or under any circumstance, including the prohibition on torture and slavery. Governments and people in authority cannot pick and choose which rights they want to honour; so, the right to free speech must go hand in hand with the right to assemble peacefully. Article 3 of the Human Rights Act argues for a critical approach to security that places human rights at the centre, reflecting on the fundamental individual security and human rights, which is an absolute ban on torture which is central to the Universal Declaration of Human Rights. The prohibition on torture or inhuman or degrading treatment is one of the few absolute rights, it is universal and it can never be justified, regardless of circumstances. It applies to every member of the human family regardless of sex, race, nationality, socio-economic group, political opinion, sexual orientation or any other status. Human rights are owed by the State to and for the people—this means public bodies must respect your human rights and the Government must ensure there are laws in place for people to understand and respecting human rights.

The consequences of child torture

All over the world, children are exploited, tortured, and killed. The governments and the political parties' leaders are responsible for supporting organisations working to end violence against children and ensuring provision of support when children reach a safe country seeking refuge. This is vital for the health of children as well as the society as whole. In examining how to prevent further trauma for children, it is important to consider how to build cohesive communities, addressing tension and promoting shared responsibility for care, and to assess how to increase reporting of difficulties by raising confidence in the social and welfare system for providing better support. In order to prevent further psychological stress for young asylum seekers it is vital to explore ways of improving operational responses and targeting vulnerable children and preventing further trauma. By developing methods to deliver a joined-up approach across the system to ensure effective integrative services will prevent much unnecessary stress.

The right to self-respect and self-worth is an integral part of psychological strength, especially for development of ego strengths and resiliency in children in the process of development. There is no dignity in the systematic degrading of children of refugees and asylum seekers lives, nor is there dignity in the failure of all our mainstream parties to stand up for their democratic principles when it comes to refugee and asylum seekers. In order to support children of refugees and asylum seekers, specifically unaccompanied children and young people, assessing risks and opportunities to understanding adolescent mental health difficulties are vital. The time-limited psychodynamic psychotherapy for adolescents and young people can prevent much of the suicide, as well as radicalisation and attraction to extremism, as the result of trauma. The knowledge of self-harm and suicidal behaviour, with an exploration of working with these issues in clinical and therapeutic practice, therefore needs to be taken into consideration within any service and police development. Recent understanding of the role of new media and peer-group processes in generating group suicidal behaviour will be discussed.

Therapeutic intervention in each session will pay particular attention to understanding self-destructive behaviour and thoughts from relational and children and adolescent developmental perspectives, and the focus on the intense emotional experience, including those who are depressed, and have self-destructive thoughts and behaviour. The focus on the developmental process and its potential deficit provides a powerful way of working therapeutically with difficulties faced by young people. In the difficult and dangerous time for unaccompanied children and young people it is vital for decision makers to consider how to progress the dynamics and work from a commitment to universal principles and civil rights for all.

According to the UN, Article 22:

> Everyone, as a member of society, has the right to social security and is entitled to realization, through national effort and international co-operation and in accordance with the organization and resources of each State, of the economic, social and cultural rights indispensable for his dignity and the free development of his personality.

On the Promotion and Protection of the Rights of Children and on Refugee Children the:

> States Parties shall take appropriate measures to ensure that a child who is seeking refugee status or who is considered a refugee in accordance with applicable international or domestic law and procedures shall, whether unaccompanied or accompanied by his or her parents or by any other person, receive appropriate protection and humanitarian assistance in the enjoyment of applicable rights set forth in the present Convention and in other international human rights or humanitarian instruments to which the said States are Parties.

Therefore the Article indicated that:

> States Parties shall provide, as they consider appropriate, co-operation in any efforts by the United Nations and other competent intergovernmental organizations or non-governmental organizations co-operating with the United Nations to protect and assist such a child and to trace the parents or other members of the family of any refugee child in order to obtain information necessary for reunification with his or her family. In cases where no parents or other members of the family can be found, the child shall be accorded the same protection as any other child permanently or temporarily deprived of his or her family environment for any reason, as set forth in the present Convention.

CHAPTER FIVE

The rule of law

In searching for a definition of the Rule of Law, I realised that there is no single universal definition. There is a need for a clear and specific definition of what constitutes torture for children. Such clarification would work towards the deliberation and prohibition of torture on children. The basic principle is that all people and institutions are subject to and accountable to law that is fairly applied to all and enforceable.

The World Justice Project stated that the Rule of Law is:

A system in which the following four universal principles are upheld:

- The government and its officials and agents as well as individuals and private entities are accountable under the law.
- The laws are clear, publicized, stable, and just; are applied evenly; and protect fundamental rights, including the security of persons and property.
- The process by which the laws are enacted, administered, and enforced is accessible, fair, and efficient.
- Justice is delivered timely by competent, ethical, and independent representatives and neutrals that are of sufficient number, have adequate resources, and reflect the makeup of the communities they serve.

These four universal principles are further developed in the following nine factors of the World Justice Project (WJP) Rule of Law Index, which measures how the rule of law is experienced by ordinary people in 99 countries around the globe. (In: http://worldjusticeproject.org/what-rule-law)

Despite the lack of a clear universal meaning of the concept of the rule of law, some issues that definitely need to be taken to considerations are the following:

- Fairness in all aspects of the law, including equality;
- Legal protections of children against dictatorship or those using and abusing; their power against children or their primary carer;
- Respect for and adherence to human rights criteria;
- Democratic participation in the decision making process;
- And review and transparency of law.

On the other hand, if we follow and define the Rule of the Law as the heart of democracy according to its structural features, we have to emphasise on the following:

- The necessity for the legitimacy of the law making process;
- Existence of an independent and effective judiciary;
- Existence of effective procedures on public office based on fairness and justice, which can be held responsible for upholding human rights and acts in accountability to independent review;
- Laws should be comprehensive, transparent, accessible, and decisive;
- Law should be legitimate in their making and manner of implementation;
- Law should be accessible to all, with a balance between the two important principles of stability and accountability.

At the international level the United Nations Security Council is the most powerful multilateral political institution, in 2013 they highlighted the transition period in societies during and after wars as one of the central issues that need consideration and that they intended as an objective of the United Nations. The report adds that the concept of Rule of Law refers to principles of ruling according to which, all people, institutions and bodies, public or private, including government itself, are answerable to law. These laws are passed in public view, implemented equally and judged in a fair manner consistent with human rights principles and criteria. United Nations Rule of Law programming extends to over 150 Member States in every region of the world.

In the same report the UN also emphasised that in at least seventy countries, a minimum of three UN entities carry out Rule of Law activities. Five or more UN entities currently work on rule of law in over thirty-five countries, seventeen of which host UN operations in peace-making, peace-keeping and peace-building. Activities support the codification, development, promotion, and implementation of international norms and standards in most fields of international law.

Therefore, there is a direct link between the Rule of Law on the one hand, and the ability of the country to confront and tackle crimes on the other. In the countries where citizens are active in the political process and laws are respected, there is little possibility that differences and oppositions may lead to violent clashes. Rule of Law guarantees law-abiding and assurance of judicial consistency of decisions, especially criminal decisions, with legal criteria. In this process, prosecutors are keepers of the law and public rights.

Having said that, and despite many universal elements present in the Rule of Law, there are differences and complexities according to different legal systems within specific contexts. Therefore, the role of the prosecutors may vary within different legal systems. Prosecutors may have a lesser or bigger role in pursuing crimes, which may lead to differences in their relations with police forces in specific countries. A close and bidirectional relation between the police and the prosecutor, especially since prosecutors rely on police for collection of evidence, is certain. In some countries, prosecutors are elected. In the UK prosecution is carried out in the name of the crown. So, the crown can prosecute and the prosecution is referred to as "the crown".

In some countries, including France, Japan, and Germany, the prosecutors are part of a career civil service. They are hired and fired by the ministry of justice and are often subject to its control. In Japan, a prosecutor can be dismissed only for reasons of health or after disciplinary proceedings. In countries, such as France, public prosecution is carried out by a single office that has representatives in courts all over the country; in Japan, too, the office of public prosecutor runs parallel to a unitary court system; in the US, states and counties have their own prosecutors and only on the federal level is the system unitary, a district attorney being appointed by the US attorney general's office for each federal district. In most US states and local jurisdictions, prosecutors are elected. On the federal level, district attorneys are members of the executive branch of the government and may be replaced when a new administration comes into office. Prosecutors, whether elected or appointed, are often subject to political pressures. Efforts have been made in Japan and Germany to insulate the office from such pressures. In both the United States and Russia the prosecutor is responsible for the police investigation, in order to ensure that the guaranteed rights of the accused are protected. In England, most prosecutions are undertaken by the police, on the basis of complaints made to them, but the more serious crimes, such as murder, are prosecuted by a legal officer of the government. The English procedure does not centralise all prosecutions for crime in a public official or department and thus differs from the system employed in Scotland and continental European countries. There is a Code for Crown Prosecutors as a public document, issued by the Director of Public Prosecutions that sets out the general principles that should be followed for making decisions. When deciding whether there is enough evidence to charge, Crown Prosecutors must consider whether evidence can be used in court and is reliable and credible.

In some systems, prosecutors are part of the judiciary instead of being under an executive person, such as the Minister of Justice. This keeps them protected and exempt from political interventions and gives them more authority to look into cases of abuse of power, while being secure from official and administrative corruptions. They therefore can be more concerned with the Rule of Law and be consistent and participatory akin with the trainings that judges will have. This kind of training provides a better quality practice and equality that professionals adopt when they perform their duties. The introduction to the UN Guidelines on the Role of Prosecutors (1990) states that the responsibility of guaranteeing that prosecutors have adequate professional training needed for their jobs is that of the government, and therefore provides a useful argument. The guidance emphasises that achieving such an objective should be through "optimal employment methods and professional and legal trainings through providing all necessary facilities needed for proper performance of prosecutors".

The Guidelines clarify that while prosecutors are under supervision themselves, they should ascertain good performance of other related bodies regarding legality of the decisions and actions they are taking. This is important for cases where the police and other security and intelligence organisations conduct their investigations in a way that might not be legal. In some legal systems, prosecutors are closely involved in investigations and in some cases play an important role in leading them, thus ascertaining and to find out with certainty the safety and health of investigations. In other systems, they only receive the evidence compiled by the police or similar bodies, and base their prosecution on that alone. A public procurator is an officer of a state charged with both the investigation and prosecution of crime. The office is a feature of a civil law inquisitorial rather than common law adversarial system. Japan, China, Russia and Indonesia use a procuratorial system and the office of a procurator is called a procuracy or procuratorate. The terms are from Latin and originate with the procurators of the Roman Empire. Despite the difference, in both systems, evidence received through illegal methods should be rejected and violators should be prosecuted (Crown Prosecution Service, 2013).

One of the most useful documents on this matter is the Constitution of Ireland (that replaced the Constitution of the Irish Free State which had been in effect since the independence of the Irish state from the United Kingdom on 6th December 1922), which in Article 38 (1937), considers all confessions, information, and evidence compiled using torture to be illegitimate and prohibited, and states that such evidence should be disregarded and the act considered punishable by law. Article 129 of Criminal Procedures referred to the detainment of a person suspected in immediate commitment of a crime and prohibits all questions based on force, lack of intentional will and deceit.

An important and concerning issue regarding the Rule of Law is the activities of organised crime groups all over the world. These groups subject people to violence, and intimidate and violate the public's primary rights populating fear and terror. Yet, violation of fundamental rights is not the only negative result of their activities; they also influence parliamentary election results and the performance of law officers, thus endangering the democratic process of law making. Organised crime groups have gained wealth and power, in many cases more than that of governments, thus gaining the capacity to influence the performance of the Rule of Law. Existence of a powerful, transparent and efficient prohibition of torture and prosecution system, together with independent and influential judges, is one method of dealing with the organised criminal activities of torturing children and their social repercussions. In this regard, prosecutors need to be equipped with the knowledge and instruments indispensable for countering organised crime against children.

Transnational relationships among organised crime groups, which use and abuse children in the form of sexual exploitation of children, child slavery, and virgin child brides sold for money, property, jewellery, and food, necessitate effective cooperation among prosecutors of different countries at the regional and international levels. To become more efficient this requires a simplification of present procedures of international cooperation, especially since we live in a world in which many traditional borders are removed to facilitate better international commercial relations, communication improvements and expansion of fiscal institutions. Despite the increasingly porous nature of borders to some degree, barriers still exist for institutions of law. Efforts by the British government in recent years to add to criminal repatriation agreements with neighbouring countries are steps forward in facilitating Rule of Law through confronting the escape of criminals. This must be further expedited and there must be joint research and investigation between transnational institutions. It is imperative to point out that at present, individual governments ultimately have the primary responsibility for preventing violence and providing effective protection and remedies, including assistance and rehabilitation support to those whose basic human rights have been violated by torture. However, due to the reprehensible, immoral, and indecent nature of child torture, and the lack of appropriate support and protections, many cases of child torture remain unreported, and torturers are often beyond the reach of any legal response and reprisal, retribution, punishment, or condemnation. One way to castigate and ensure reprimand of torturers and to help prevent reoccurrence of child torture is through public awareness and civic society engagement to take action, and measures to implement appropriate practical procedures against torture in general, and specifically torture of children.

Torturing in general and torturing children in particular, is a serious act of terrorising a child. In Article 3 of the Universal Declaration of Human Rights (1948), terrorism is considered a violation of the fundamental human right of a person to have life, freedom, and security. The introduction to the Declaration denounces disregard and violations of human rights that would lead to brutal and severe acts of retaliation and violence. The objectives of the Universal Declaration of

Human Rights are to reach a world in which all people are free from fear. This right is emphasised in the introduction to the International Charter of Economic, Social and Cultural Rights and the International Charter on Social and Political Rights. Fear of terrorism sometimes leads to an imbalance in regimes which are subject to it. These regimes will often go against democratic forces in favour of dictatorial forces and thus are sternly destructive to the Rule of Law. Sometimes, the methods and manner used in torturing children are similar to terrorist activity, despite the fact that most regimes and organisations inflicting torture claim that their primary concerns are safety and security and freedom for all. In torturing children, indeed adults too, they show brutality against democracy, violate basic human rights and commit crimes against humanity.

Looking at Article 3, that is an absolute right prohibiting torture, and inhumane or degrading treatment or punishment, the state must not itself engage in torture, or in inhumane or degrading treatment. It is also obliged to prevent such treatment happening, and to carry out an investigation into allegations that it has. The state must comply with its obligations within its territory and, in exceptional circumstances, in different countries where it exercises effective jurisdiction. The prohibition on torture has been part of the British common law framework since the eighteenth century. Today the legal framework around torture is considerably more sophisticated. It is prohibited both by civil law and by several Acts of Parliament. The UK has also ratified several international conventions prohibiting torture and ill-treatment. This framework is supported by an institutional structure of regulators, including the Care Quality Commission (CQC), the Independent Police Complaints Commission (IPCC) and Her Majesty's Chief Inspectorate of Prisons for England and Wales (HMI Prisons).

People who use health and social care services have a right to be protected from inhumane and degrading treatment and when there are allegations of mistreatment the state has an obligation to investigate. There is evidence of mistreatment of some users of health and social care services that breaches Article 3. A review by the Equality and Human Rights Commission shows that:

- People who are receiving health or social care from private and voluntary sector providers do not have the same level of direct protection under the Human Rights Act as those receiving it from public bodies;

- Local authorities do not make the most effective use of the scope that they have for protecting and promoting human rights when commissioning care from other providers;
- Better inspections of all care settings are needed.

This review reports that children detained in young offender institutions and in the secure training centres, indeed secure children's homes, are under the full control of the authorities, as the result the responsibilities and accountability of the state are greater. Because of the vulnerability of young people in these circumstances the border on of the seriousness for defining torture, inhumane or degrading treatment or punishment is lowered. The review stated that:

- There is evidence that restraint is used extensively, but better data are needed.
- Authorised restraint techniques used in young offender institutions and secure training centres do not meet human rights standards.
- The use of restraint as a form of discipline, rather than in cases of absolute necessity or safety, is in breach of Article 3.
- Possible breaches of Article 3 in these settings are not always effectively investigated. (PP 71)

The absolute prohibition on torture is included in many national and international treaties, such as the International Covenant on Civil and Political Rights (ICCPR) Article 7, the United Nations Convention Against Torture (UNCAT) and the European Convention Against Torture (ECPT) ratified by the United Kingdom. Freedom from torture and inhumane or degrading treatment or punishment therefore is an absolute right that should be applied even during a war or in times of threat to national security. States should never, under any circumstances, adjourn, postpone or deviate from the rule of law and set of conditions from Article 3, be it for public order purposes or in the name interest of the general public, or due to threats to national security. Under Article 3 every person has a right to protection regardless of their race, religious, identity or actions. So, any action beyond this will be considered a breach of Article 3, whether the level of torture or other human rights violations and inhumane or degrading treatment or punishment in any circumstances of any case. The more vulnerable the person is the more likely it is that a minimum harshness and sternness will affect the psychological and physical health of the person and this will be severe in cases of children being tortured. The assessment of the minimum level therefore is relative and depends on the circumstances of the case including the duration of torture, the physical and psychological effects and the sex, age and state of health of the children young person or adult. One of the challenges is the child's inability to talk about what has happened to her or him and to articulate and communicate coherently, or communicate at all, about how he or she is being affected by any particular treatment. Despite this, measures taken in certain countries to counter terrorism have led to serious worries regarding human rights violations and the rights and protection of children and young people. To counter this horrible and dangerous phenomenon, it is important to work towards the recognition of the Rule of Law and insist on primary principles of criminal procedures. No governments or other organisations openly claim that they see fit to torture children for any other reasons. The former UN Secretary General, Kofi Annan, said in his speech on 3rd March 2003, to the Anti-Terrorism Committee of the UN Security Council, that we must have a plan for international action according to our obligation of defending the Rule of Law. He commented that since terrorism is based on the calculated use of violence in order to violate the Rule of Law, our reaction should be in line with the Rule of Law. Similar proposals and recommendations for the purpose of respecting human rights and honouring the Rule of Law have been put forward by prosecutors and other sources. In their anti-terrorism efforts, the UN General Assembly ratified such proposals with resolution number 50/195 on 20th December 2004 and the office of the UN Human Rights Council (UNHRC) followed suit in September 2003. UNHRC has formed and obliged a subcommittee to promote and support human rights through detailed regulations in anti-terrorism acts. In addition, the European Council in 2005 issued directives on human rights and anti-terrorism, according to which all state activities against terrorism should be based on the Rule of Law and respect for human rights, and all racism, prejudice or despotism should be avoided in these actions. Furthermore, there are needs to ensure these with adequate supervision in place to prevent autocracy. In the same line, the International Bar Association, in 2003, emphasised the two fundamental principles with regard to confronting terrorism, indicating that the threat of terrorism should not be used by states as an excuse to disregard essential international laws, and states should not use confrontation with terrorism as a pretext to illegally limit the rights of expression, religion, etc.

Despite all this work in developing law and security, unfortunately the torture of children is still widely practiced in many parts of the world. As a result many children of refugees and unaccompanied minors may carry aggressions and in their youth act out the humiliation and pain they have endured. They may feel rejected in their new society, especially if they feel they have been left without appropriate care.

A case of radicalisation

An important example is the 15th of April 2013, when two coordinated Improvised Explosive Devices exploded near the finish line of the Boston Marathon. The fatalities were low but the symbolism was high and was compared to 9/11. The bombers, Tamerlan and Dzhokhar Tsarnaev, had planned on killing and dying in the name of the global Jihad. They were self-radicalised home grown terrorists, and while they were inspired by militant jihadism and in loose contact with terrorists in Dagestan, they operated alone.

The following is evidence of the radicalisation process that led to these two young men adopting violent jihad. The Tsarnaev brothers with their family came from the war-torn Chechen Diaspora and found asylum in the United States. The elder brother, Tamerlan, carried actual memories of fleeing from the Chechen war in the 1990s. He lived in Dagestan for a year at the time when the Chechen warlord Basayev was engaging in a campaign of more than thirty suicide attacks, including mass hostage takings. Their mother was persecuted for not covering herself according to the Islamic rules. All evidence presented by the media indicated that when Tamerlan went to the US, he tried to assimilate but clearly he failed to make it. The family struggled hard to make a living and as a result of hardships the parents divorced and the father returned to Dagestan. Dzhokhar, the younger brother, made it into an American university but Tamerlan did not succeed in higher education, trying to pursue a boxing career instead. When his immigration status precluded a boxing career, he became disillusioned, feeling rejected by the society that he felt close to and belonged to at that point. Meanwhile, his mother raised a concern about him smoking marijuana and drinking alcohol. To help him, she arranged an Islamic tutor for him. The ingredients for the lethal cocktail of terrorism came together when Tamerlan's individual vulnerabilities made him seek online contacts via the internet and brought him in touch with offline mentors, militants, and extremists who glorified Al-Qaeda's global jihad. Through these channels he became receptive to the terrorist ideology, found a jihadist group with global reach to align with, received technical instructions from the Inspire magazine and found enough support for executing the Boston marathon attack, pulling his younger brother along and dying in the process as he had expected. Given this level of dissolution, despair, and anger, one cannot help but wonder how these two young people's lives would have turned out, if only the older brother's immigration problem would not have created such humiliation, despair, and rejection of the society that he desired to become a boxing champion for. One can question whether prevention of this could have resulted in the prevention of so much pain and suffering that has been caused to so many innocent people in the Boston bombing and their family and friends.

The International Commission of Lawyers, in its Berlin Declaration of 2004, accepts terrorist threats as against human rights, and reminds prosecutors that their responsibility to uphold human rights doubles during critical times when the Rule of Law and human rights are not certain or guaranteed. The Declaration (2004) emphasises that the authority should reject evidence compiled in a way that is contrary to human rights and recognises the right of innocence and a fair trial for all the accused, as well as stresses that violators of these principles should be prosecuted. Accordingly, violators of law, including organised crime and terrorist groups, should not force prosecutors into taking revenge or responding with similar acts. Looking at the Quran, the holy book of Muslims, it states: "Those who believe, raise for god and confess in justice and there is not privilege for the people who do not spread justice. Spread justice, this is closer to belief." Interpretation of this is dangerous for a young man who feel rejected.

This leads to radicalisation and sadly to such fanatic action. Radicalisation is the process by which young people become attracted to and become extreme in their way of thinking and, in some cases, then participate in extremist fanatic activity. Extremism, as long as it is only vocal or active, as in the form of demonstrations or talk of opposition to British or Western values within the rule of law, can be considered as individual liberty and mutual respect and tolerance of different faiths. But, if the extreme beliefs increase to the level of becoming violent in the form of a suicide bomber or killing members of the opposition or armed forces, then it becomes terrorist activity and is beyond extreme thinking.

There is need for specialist services which consists of processes for responding to identified risk and need, and having provision of appropriate support and to deliver an appropriate response to support preventions when potential issues are identified by parents, friends, peers, teachers or other professionals. The Children's Services and the Lead Member for Children's Services need to establish a range of principles in relation to children's safeguarding which extends across the ordinary child protection agenda in relation to the safeguarding and wellbeing of children and young people with regard to radicalism.

There is a complex relationship between the various aspects of a child or young person's identity which determines their vulnerability in general, and indeed their attraction to extremism, and that might be influenced by demographics and poverty indicators that are consistently overlooked as vulnerabilities within a timeframe when they can be addressed. This in many cases will increase the ability of extremists to exploit, operate, and recruit young people who may feel distant and alien from cultural and religious norms and uncomfortable with their place in the society and people around them. There are many basic and well known factors leading young people to join extremism, including family tensions, sense of isolation, adolescence, low self-esteem, disassociating from existing friendship group and becoming involved with a new and different group of friends, searching for answers to questions about identity, faith and belonging, migration, immigration status, the local community tensions, events affecting their country or region of origin, alienation from UK and Western cultures and values, having a sense of grievance that is triggered by personal experience of racism and discriminations or indeed aspects of Government policy, perceptions of injustice, feelings of failure, rejection of civic life, past experiences of imprisonment and torture, poor resettlement and lack of reintegration, previous involvement with weapons and fighting groups, and easy access to extremism. Other reasons are due to the fact that they associate directly with known individuals attached to extreme groups or because they are in or around locations where these extreme individuals actively promote their activities. Another point of contact to extremism is via the internet, access to or distribution of extremist material, contacts made covertly via extremist literature/other media material likely to incite racial and religious hatred or acts of violent propaganda, or fundraising to support groups with links to extremist activity. There are other aspects such as the child or young person's encounters with peer, social, family or faith group rejection and those who can easily access extremist ideological, political or religious influence within or outside the UK and other countries the young person is living.

It is important to recognise that many young people may be emotionally affected by the troubles happening around the world, specifically in areas of conflict, and of course the influence of media, which shows images of children dying of hunger and dehydration, increases the emotional response. However, this is different from children and young people that are active sympathisers or supporters of extremist activity. There are correlations between extremists and the personal experience of poverty and social isolation due to the young person's identity. Young people in disadvantaged positions who might feel discriminated against are more vulnerable to extreme groups. Social isolation and exclusion due to a lack of meaningful education or employment appropriate to their skills contributes more to young people's social isolation, identity conflict, and confusion. Some of these insecurities and identity confusions are quite commonly associated with the process of development.

For instance, a young asylum seeker who is awaiting a decision on his or her immigration matter would have extreme anxiety and insecurity about his or her future. Such feelings are an existential anxiety. An unaccompanied child may have even more conflicted emotion due to absent family and loving relationships in their life. This is in addition to trauma they have endured in their lives, particularly trauma associated with torture, war, religious or sectarian conflict.

Immigration status and awaiting the outcome of asylum claims for young refugees is a challenging matter that intrudes and interferes with young people's lives, such as educational achievements, and these may lead to psychological problems. Young people can experience a constant underlying anxiety in relation to immigration issue and this will affect their ability to settle and integrate and can compromise their educational achievement. Children and young people do not have knowledge about their immigration status and may not understand the limited information that may be available to them. For unaccompanied young people concerns with their immigration status is a serious factor in their life that affecting their ways of thinking and feeling about their future. Those concerns are related to the sense of security or lack of it for many refugee children who may have witnessed their family members being raped, tortured, and murdered, and in some cases they have been tortured and severely abused themselves. Young unaccompanied asylum seekers may have been raped and have experienced the disappearance or imprisonment of family members, have had to flee from their homes, often on their own, and will have travelled through a number of countries. Some children and young people also come to this country due to living in situations of serious poverty and deprivation; some may have arrived in this country as a result of being trafficked for exploitation in the sex industry and found themselves being exploited in the UK.

Some children and young refugees arrive with parents or with other relatives. Some of these children and young people live with parents who are unable to respond to their needs and living in an inadequate or abusive environment due to their parent/s own emotional problems as a result of the trauma they have endured in the past. Some are living with relatives whom they do not know, others are looked after by social services, and many young people are living alone. So, the young refugees have a wide range of needs: emotional, physical, social, economic, and, in some cases, psychological, which require help with mental ill-health in a timely manner. Their experiences need to be understood in order to assist them to ease the process of settlement and integration, and to develop or regain some resilience and build a sense of stability to develop hope and aspirations within their new environment.

Thinking of such varieties of reasons that a child or young person might be influenced by extremists, there is the important question of why? Why do so many young people, whether born Muslim or converted into Islam, have so much aggression and what are the reasons that they engage in acts of killing and terrorising others? This is not to suggest that there are justifications for aggressive acts, and of course ending their own life, or that people should take law into their own hands and punish what feels wrong to or for them. Having said this, it is a question for civil society to look at for potentially helpful answers if we are looking to remedy these inhumane acts of retaliation and radicalisation.

The protection and needs of refugee children and young people are not considered in the Protection of Children Act (1989), although reference is made in relation to Black and minority ethnic communities and a suggestion has been made that Black families are more likely to be subjected to child protection investigations, and receive less family support services if they are in need.

The policy and legislative agenda around children and young people is undergoing changes by the government agenda of eradicating child poverty by 2020, and creating an inclusive society for all children in the UK. The Every Child Matters (2003) set out five areas in which the government says outcomes for children must be monitored.

These are: 1. Being healthy, 2. Staying safe, 3. Enjoying and achieving, 4. Making a positive contribution, 5. Economic well-being. Every Child Matters states as next steps an aim of ensuring that there is "the right balance between national standards and local flexibility" (2004, p. 18). However, there is little mention of refugee and asylum-seeking children and young people within the document. There are limited references to issues that may affect refugee young people (such as support for bilingual learners in school), and in relation to unaccompanied young people there are proposals regarding dealing with trafficking and dispersal of this group. This is despite the fact that this group are one of the worst affected in the UK by child poverty levels due to asylum and immigration legislation currently being tightened. The UK government continues to maintain its reservation on the UNCRC, and immigration issues continue to take precedence over the best interests of the child. Whilst the reservation remains in force we have a two tier system, one tier of children for whom their best interests are the paramount consideration and another for those asylum seekers and refugee children and young people whose best interests are a secondary consideration. It would be helpful if the Government can eliminate this double standard which directly violates the human rights of children affected by immigration legislation. Such a change can and would provide clarity on the care of refugee children, so that they receive equal treatment and support to other children, who are not subject to immigration control, when their basic human rights are violated. Such clarification would also provide clearer guidance for professionals in the field, indeed eliminating many unnecessary anxieties for young refugees and asylum seekers.

Another issue that can influence ideas of justice and impartiality specifically for children of refugees is the media's approach and the pressure that children might feel under indirectly. This can lead the young refugee to feel rejected and unwanted, leading them to make the decision that the society that she or he is living in is not just and adequate, and that there are no fair procedures in place to meet their needs. These decisions by young people might gratify the desire of a whole host of people for a while, but the negative and long term effect of such societal attitudes can be traumatic for children of refugees and further alienate them, as well as adversely affect their developmental processes to grow to be a positive member of society.

Avoiding an unhealthy negative media atmosphere can therefore influence a healthier developmental process and prevent much pain of rejection for adolescents. Although there have been criticisms in more recent years about the exploitation and distortion of reality in the media, especially since the death of Princess Diana, it seems that regulations and principles that should be honoured for the greater good of public interests are still greatly overlooked. The refugee issues are the ones that are frequently used by the media in a negative manner.

> The appearance of commercial media on the scene of information has strongly affected the way in which the media report happenings to the point that it affects their initial purpose. Indeed, whereas in the past media has had a strong informative/educational intent, more recently we have borne witness to an increasing commitment of media to serve entertainment purposes, therefore provoking what media specialists have defined as a switch from information to "infotainment": information-based media content or programming that also includes entertainment content in an effort to enhance popularity with audiences and consumers. (Demers, 2005)

However, all of the above discussion outlines the problems and the robust capacity of the Rule of Law to mediate injustice while also addressing the unresolved ambiguities and in some cases exploitation and depravity present in many systems that undermine the underlying objectives of such institutions. Another example is in terms of child protection, specifically in the set of circumstances of children of refugees who are increasingly more vulnerable and susceptible to violation of their rights. The way in which law is adopted and implemented is a central issue that needs attention at local, regional, national, and international levels. Although the matter is far more complex and cannot be stated clearly in the scope of this book, it is important to bring attention to the fact that without independent and transparent legal structures in place within individual nations, as well as international exchange and monitoring, working towards states upholding their obligation to human rights in general and the protection of children more specifically will remain challenging. The movement towards greater realisation of justice for children who are tortured and deprived of their basic rights therefore will become undeveloped, apathetic, and indifferent. As a result, legal structures to protect children from torture and other forms of human right violations will remain ineffective, ambiguous and not well-defined. Urgent action is needed in this area in order to continue the momentum of positive change around the issue of torture which will lead to the elimination of torture once and for all.

CHAPTER SIX

The European Convention on Human Rights

Article 3 of the European Convention on Human Rights (ECHR) states that, "No one shall be subjected to torture or inhuman or degrading treatment or punishment" (1950a). Under Article 3 a person can make a claim for protection based directly on Article 3 of ECHR as states are prohibited from returning a person to a country where they may suffer a violation of their rights.

Furthermore, Article 8 (1950b) of the ECHR states that: "Everyone has the right to respect for his private and family life, his home and his correspondence." Article 8 issues may be raised as part of an asylum application, or in the context of an appeal against deportation or removal. Article 8 is a qualified rather than an absolute right and the second part of it sets out circumstances where authorities may interfere with the right. The Immigration Rules amendment in 2012 provides clarifications on the qualified nature of Article 8.

Article 31 of the 1951 Refugee Convention prohibits states from penalising a refugee for illegal entry when the purpose of their entry is to claim asylum. The UN Convention on the Rights of the Child (UNCRC) is particularly relevant as separated children are some of the most vulnerable people in society. The relevant article is Article 22 emphasising that:

1. States Parties shall take appropriate measures to ensure that a child who is seeking refugee status or who is considered a refugee in accordance with applicable international or domestic law and procedures shall, whether unaccompanied or accompanied by his or her parents or by any other person, receive appropriate protection and humanitarian assistance in the enjoyment of applicable rights set forth in the present Convention and in other international human rights or humanitarian instruments to which the said States are Parties.

2. For this purpose, States Parties shall provide, as they consider appropriate, co-operation in any efforts by the United Nations and other competent intergovernmental organizations or non-governmental organizations co-operating with the United Nations to protect and assist such a child and to trace the parents or other members of the family of any refugee child in order to obtain information necessary for reunification with his or her family. In cases where no parents or other members of the family can be found, the child shall be accorded the same protection as any other child permanently or temporarily deprived of his or her family environment for any reason, as set forth in the present Convention.

The Convention on the Rights of the Child

The Convention on the Rights of the Child of Part II and International Human Rights System stated that there, "is concerned with protecting children from injury and providing disabled children adequate protection." Article 2 states that the rights set forth in the Convention must be applied "[…] without discrimination of any kind, irrespective of […] disability"; the Article 4 concerns the right to life and Article 19 provides for the protection of "[…] the child from all forms of physical or mental violence, injury or abuse, neglect or negligent treatment, maltreatment or exploitation, including sexual abuse […]". The central provision of Convention concerning the rights of disabled children is Article 23 that indicates that, "States Parties recognise that a mentally or physically disabled child should enjoy a full and decent life, in conditions which ensure dignity, promote self-reliance and facilitate the child's active participation in the community."

Article 23 further emphasises on provision of assistance to the child and those responsible for his or her care, stating that:

> [...] shall be designed to ensure that the disabled child has effective access to and receives education, training, health care services, rehabilitation services, preparation for employment and recreation opportunities in a manner conducive to the child's achieving the fullest possible social integration and individual development.

According to Article 23 (3) and Article 23 (4) services for disabled children should, wherever possible, be provided free of charge indicating that States Parties shall promote, "The exchange of appropriate information in the field or preventative health care and of medical, psychological and functional treatment of disabled children." Article 24 (2) (d) of the Convention also is relevant to the prevention of disabilities in the part emphasising that, "States Parties undertake to ensure appropriate prenatal and post-natal health care for mothers."

Although disability of many children of refugees may result from torture and abuse, the directly related Article regarding torture of children, Article 37, focuses on the Deprivation of Liberty suggesting that it is the responsibility of States Parties to ensure:

   (a) No child shall be subjected to torture or other cruel, inhuman or degrading treatment or punishment. Neither capital punishment nor life imprisonment without possibility of release shall be imposed for offences committed by persons below eighteen years of age;

   (b) No child shall be deprived of his or her liberty unlawfully or arbitrarily. The arrest, detention or imprisonment of a child shall be in conformity with the law and shall be used only as a measure of last resort and for the shortest appropriate period of time;

   (c) Every child deprived of liberty shall be treated with humanity and respect for the inherent dignity of the human person, and in a manner which takes into account the needs of persons of his or her age. In particular, every child deprived of liberty shall be separated from adults, unless it is considered in the child's best interest not to do so, and shall have the right

to maintain contact with his or her family through correspondence and visits, save in exceptional circumstances;

(d) Every child deprived of his or her liberty shall have the right
to prompt access to legal and other appropriate assistance, as
well as the right to challenge the legality of the deprivation of
his or her liberty before a court or other competent, independent and impartial authority, and to a prompt decision on any
such action.

Article 39 emphasises the appropriate measures that States should take
to promote physical and psychological recovery as well as provision
for social reintegration of a child who has been neglected, subjected
to exploitation, torture or abuse by any other form of cruel, inhuman
or degrading treatment or punishment, or armed conflicts. Article 39
states that:

Such recovery and reintegration shall take place in an environment
which fosters the health, self-respect and dignity of the child. The
obligation to ensure that in all actions concerning children, the best
interests of the child shall be a primary consideration can be demonstrated by adherence to section 55 of the Borders, Citizen and
Immigration Act 2009.

The statutory duty to safeguard and promote the welfare of children
in the UK in the guidelines emphasise that the case workers need to be
aware of Section 55 of the Borders, Citizen and Immigration Act 2009. It
is therefore the statutory duty of the Home Secretary to make arrangements to ensure that UKBA functions and services carried out by third
parties on UKBA's behalf have regard for the need to safeguard and
promote the welfare of children who are in the United Kingdom. This
statutory duty is related to the children in the UK and those dealing
with asylum applications for children. Consequently case workers dealing with children need to ensure they are familiar with the approach for
Arrangements to Safeguard and Promote the Welfare of Children in the
process of carrying out their functions, including immigration control.
The Statutory Guidance to the UKBA on making arrangements to safeguard and promote the welfare of children, issued under section 55, sets
out the key provisions for safeguarding and promoting the welfare of
children as they apply both generally to public bodies who deal with
children (Part 1), and specifically to the UKBA (Part 2). Any person

exercising immigration, asylum, nationality, and customs functions are required to have regard for the following principles:

- Every child matters, even for children who are subject to immigration control;
- The best interests of the child are to be a primary concern in decisions affecting children;
- Ethnic identity, language, religion, faith, gender, and disability are to be taken into account when working with a child and their family;
- Children should be consulted and the wishes and feelings of children taken into account, wherever practicable, when decisions affecting them are made. Where parents and carers are present, they will have primary responsibility for the children's concerns;
- Children should have their applications dealt with in a way that minimises the uncertainty that they may experience.

Coming back to The International Convention, Article 19 of the Convention on the Rights of the Child requires states to take:

> […] all appropriate legislative, administrative, social and educational measures to protect the child from all forms of physical or mental violence, injury or abuse, neglect or negligent treatment, maltreatment or exploitation including sexual abuse, while in the care of parent(s), legal guardian(s) or any other person who has the care of the child […]. (UNICEF, "Violence against Children in West and Central Africa", p. 16)

Since its adoption in 1989 and after more than sixty years of advocacy, the United Nations Convention on the Rights of the Child has been ratified by more governments (all except Somalia and the US) than any other human rights instrument. The Convention is also the only international human rights treaty that expressly gives non-governmental organisations (NGOs) a role in monitoring its implementation under Article 45a. (UN Convention on the Rights of the Child, A/RES/44/25, dated 20th November 1989)

The basic premise of the Convention on the Rights of the Child is that children (all human beings under the age of eighteen) are born with fundamental freedoms and the inherent rights of all human beings. Many governments have enacted legislation, created mechanisms and put into place a range of creative measures to ensure the protection and realisation of the rights of those under the age of eighteen. Each government must also report back on children's rights in their country.

The Committee on the Rights of the Child is the monitoring body to the Convention on the Rights of the Child (CRC). The Committee holds regular meetings and oversees the progress made by States Parties in fulfilling their obligations. It can make suggestions and recommendations to governments and the General Assembly on ways to meet the Convention's objectives. Under revised Sections 17 and 20 of the Children Act 2004 (s22 & s93 of the Children Act 1995 in Scotland) local authorities in England and Wales have a duty to make available and be responsible for the support for unaccompanied asylum-seeking children. Section 17 places a general duty on every local authority to safeguard and promote the welfare of children in need in general, including children of refugees and asylum seekers, whether accompanied or unaccompanied, within their area by providing services appropriate to the need of the individual children. Further, Section 20 requires every local authority to arrange for accommodation for children in need within their area who require accommodation if:

- There is no person who has parental responsibility for them;
- The children have been lost or abandoned; or
- The person who has been caring for them has not been able to provide them with suitable accommodation.

The Local Authority's assessment of the individual child's needs is the basis on which the authority will provide suitable accommodation and other related support. In England, this assessment and support will be the responsibility of the Children's Services departments within Local Authority and in Wales and Scotland, within the Local Authorities' Social Services departments.

The Universal Declaration of Human Rights can be, and is in some cases, interpreted differently by different states, authorities, politicians, policy makers, and other people around the world. Therefore, the perception of rights changes according to geography, culture and politics, making it difficult to have a universal shared understanding to protect Human Rights including children rights for everyone, everywhere.

Human rights violations today, remain systematic and widespread. Oppressive governments continue to suppress dissenting opinions and maintain political control, resulting in an arbitrary and abusive judicial regime in many parts of the world. The lack of accountability within governments means that abuses by officials can go ahead often without proper monitoring and evaluation. Some of the most common abuses include arbitrary detention, torture, and ill-treatment of prisoners; severe restrictions on freedom of expression and association; violations of women and children; control on independent thinking, aimed at particular political parties or opposition groups, and on free speech. For the purposes of this book, my focus is on the torture of children of refugees and its impact on those individuals.

The UK's position

The UK Government has a reservation on Article 22 of the UNCRC, which it argues is necessary in the interests of effective immigration control, but the Government also states that the reservation does not prevent the UK from having regard to the Convention in its care and treatment of children. It states that, in practice, "the interests of asylum-seeking children and young people are fully respected" in particular under the Human Rights Act 1998 and that, "notwithstanding the Reservation, there are sufficient social and legal mechanisms in place to ensure that children receive a generous level of protection and care whilst they are in the UK". The reservation is justified by the Government as necessary to prevent the Convention affecting immigration status. The Joint Committee on Human Rights, Twenty-sixth Report of Session 2005–2006 states:

> Our principal concern is that the practical impact of the reservation goes far beyond the determination of immigration status, and leaves children subject to immigration control with a lower level of protection in relation to a range of rights which are unrelated to their immigration status.

The Joint Committee report further concludes:

> We are disappointed that the Government has failed to act on our earlier recommendation that it should withdraw the immigration and nationality reservation to the CRC. In our view, the maintenance of this reservation, which withdraws the protection of the Convention from a particularly vulnerable group of children, undermines

the otherwise strong record of the Government in the advancement of children's rights, and calls into question the UK's commitment to a Convention central to international human rights protection. We reiterate our previous recommendation that the Government should withdraw this reservation.

In addition the Committee stated in their Report on Human Trafficking:

> [...] Evidence submitted to us emphasised the potential conflict between UK immigration and asylum policy and child protection principles, which dictate that the primary consideration is the best interests of the child [...]. The previous JCHR pressed the Government to remove this reservation and in our view the need for this to be done is further strengthened by its potential effect on child trafficking victims if their best interests are not to be compromised.

However, Section 55 of the Nationality, Immigration and Asylum Act (2002) gives the Home Secretary power to deny support to asylum seekers who have not applied for asylum "as soon as reasonably practicable". In December 2003, the Home Secretary announced that asylum seekers would be considered to have made their claim "as soon as reasonably practicable" if they could give "credible explanation" of how they arrived in the UK within three days of applying for asylum. Section 55 of the Nationality, Immigration and Asylum Act (2002) gives the Home Office power to deny support to asylum seekers deemed not to have applied for asylum "as soon as reasonably practicable". The Section 55 of the Borders Citizenship and Immigration Act (2009) requires the Home Office to make arrangements to safeguard and promote the welfare of children in discharging its immigration and nationality functions. However, the Section 57 of the Nationality, Immigration and Asylum Act (2002) states that Home Office support can be withheld if the asylum seeker fails to provide complete or accurate information to the authorities or fails to co-operate with further enquiries.

The Dublin III Regulation provides all EU member states with a mechanism for allocating responsibility to a single member state for processing an asylum claim. A number of principles apply, such as family unity the state where the person first entered the EU is responsible for dealing with an asylum claim. Therefore, appropriate support needs to be provided for the applicant preventing the person from living in inhuman or degrading circumstances. This is in line with the National Assistance Act 1948 which gives local authorities the responsibility to provide accommodation and services to people with a disability or other care needs. It also puts an obligation on local authorities to conduct an assessment of anyone who might require residential care. From 1996 to December 1999, destitute in-country asylum seekers were supported by local authorities under the terms of this Act. However, Section 9 of the Asylum & Immigration (Treatment of Claimants, etc.) Act 2004 gives the Home Office power to withdraw support from families with children aged under eighteen whose asylum application and appeals have been rejected and who are thought not to be co-operating with efforts to remove them. It also prevents local authorities from providing such support for the whole family although they may have the power to provide support to the child.

The Home Office published figures (2012) for hate crimes which indicated that around 44,000 incidents of hate crimes that were reported to the police in 2011–2012, of which eighty-two per cent were race related. The Government acknowledged that hate crime is underreported and the actual number is likely to be higher. The Government Code of Practice for Victims of Crime (December 2013) sets out the information and services that people affected by crime will receive from criminal justice agencies in England and Wales. It indicates that the Government is committed to enhancing services for "victims" of the most serious crimes, including "victims" of hate crimes and those persistently targeted, vulnerable or intimidated, aggrieved, and injured. However refugee children and young people as a group of potentially vulnerable are not addressed for such protections.

Further the Crime Persecution Service published three key documents in 2014: "Hate crime strategy" (May 2014); "Hate crime delivery plan" (October 2014); and concerned by the lack of progress made in prosecuting disability hate crime, "Disability hate crime—Crime Persecution Service action plan".

These should be taken seriously by local authorities, police, legal professionals, health services, mental health services, and other professionals in statutory and voluntary sector, and other key stakeholders for the protections of refugee children and young people. Stakeholders should constantly examine how to build on the developments for a better system and approach to identify steps to tackle hate crime in all its forms and in every local community, including for refugee children and young people. It is important to build cohesive communities, addressing tension and promoting shared values based on human rights, and to increase equality in practice that raises confidence in the criminal justice system while providing culturally appropriate support for children in need to reclaim their dignity, self-respect, and self-worth.

According to the UK Home Office and its MI5's agency, radicalisation is defined as: "The process by which people come to support terrorism and violent extremism and, in some cases, then join terrorist groups." *The Guardian* newspaper on 20th August 2008 reported that the MI5 report identified those at risk of radicalisation, those who recruit them, and what can be done to prevent radicalisation. *The Guardian* article suggests that no single measure will reduce radicalisation in the UK and that the only way to combat it is by targeting at-risk vulnerable groups and trying to assimilate them into society. This may include helping young people find jobs, better integrating immigrant populations into the local culture, and effectively reintegrating ex-prisoners into society. The key vulnerabilities identified by MI5 analysts that made those studied receptive to extremist ideology included the experience of migrating to the UK and facing marginalisation and racism; the failure of those with degrees to achieve anything but low-grade jobs; a serious criminal past; travel abroad for up to six months at a time and contact with extremist networks overseas; and religious naivety. The report suggests that the relationship between criminality and radicalisation is complex, with some criminals attracted by the violent aspects of terrorism, while others with a criminal past felt genuine regret for their activities. MI5 says that, "Some appeared to have turned to violent extremist groups in the misguided belief that participation in jihad might help atone for previous wrongdoing." There are some suggestions, such as those by McCauley and Mosalenko (2009), which indicate that:

> Disproportionate involvement in risk taking and status seeking is particularly true of those young men who come from disadvantaged family backgrounds, have lower IQ levels, are of lower socioeconomic status, and who therefore have less opportunity to succeed in society along a traditional career path. These young men are more likely to be involved in gang activity, violent crime, and other high-risk behaviour.

While there is hope in that some resources have been allocated and there are programs being implemented, there is still a huge need for appropriate services for the children of refugee and asylum seekers in order to achieve positive outcomes. So, there seems to be a very slow prospect for change from within, leaving particular obligation and accountability of governments and responsible services to remain unchallenged. Within this context, additional initiatives and actions need to be taken that are specifically aimed at issues that children of refugee and asylum seekers face when engaging professional networks. We need to reflect on the difficulties that arise when these issues are raised in public, and discuss how to counteract those framings in reality.

CHAPTER SEVEN

Children and mental health

The mental health of children of refugees can be affected by experiences of loss, separation, stress, and the various psychological impacts of uncertainties brought about by the refugee experience, including attempts to integrate into a new society and culture. The psychological impact of life in the host country, i.e., the UK, can be both positive and negative. The relief associated with newly found safety and access to food, shelter, education, and other opportunities not previously available to some people is naturally significant. Having said this, often politicians, and other relevant professionals, even social workers overlook or fail to ascertain the extreme challenges that are also entailed in starting a new life as a refugee. Evidence indicates concerns resulting from broken attachments and displacement especially affect children's mental health, with one of the major risk factors being sudden separation from familiar environments. Data from my work at the Refugee Therapy Centre during the last sixteen years and, prior to that, in other charity and community organisations for many years, as well as in the NHS, managing children and family referrals, shows increased levels of psychological ill health among children of refugees, especially post-traumatic stress, depression, social anxiety, withdrawal, and on occasion outbursts of anger. The principles underlying the delivery of mental health care for these children are almost non-existent, as are necessary systematic support and preventions that can be undertaken in the school context, also in the Child and Adolescences Mental Health Service (CAMHS), Social services, and other approved services in the community.

It is important to note that some key aspects of British Immigration Rules create insecurity and further stress when children reach adult age. This is a clear tension between the law and the best interests of the child as a primary principle for a healthier society. Day after day in our practice at the Refugee Therapy Centre we confront such difficulties and develop particular concern for the plight of unaccompanied children and lack of attention to the mental health needs of this vulnerable group.

Within the host country, the previous dangers from which a refugee child has fled, either with family or unaccompanied may no longer be present. However, the stress and potential traumatisation incurred through the asylum-seeking process as well as social isolation brought about by language barriers and other consequences of social rejection (including prejudice, racism, xenophobia, inaccessible services and care, and cultural bewilderment) often exact extreme costs for children of refugees. Moreover, the additional anxiety produced by inadequate or unstable social and caring structures such as foster homes, state custody, poor housing and poverty can leave lasting psychological and emotional effects without proper attention and intervention.

It is a well-known fact that trauma plays a significant part in the psychogenesis of violence (e.g., Johnson, Cohen, Brown, Smailes, & Bernstein, 1999). After suffering multiple traumas during their lives, children of refugees and immigrants in general may develop some psychological difficulties. For children of refugees who endured trauma and come to this country with hope and expectation—the related immigrations and other organisational conditions in the host country can adversely affect their psychological well-being. These certainly hinder the process of children adaptation and integration in the host country. There is therefore a need to think about and search for appropriate help for the efficient integration of refugee children and young people in the host country.

Children do not have the developed personality or psychological structures necessary to deal with the horrors and trauma of torture. They are not prepared to be separated from their parents, assume false identities, hide with strangers or witness such cruelty, suffering and death that define many brutal environments where systematic human rights violations occur. Childhood traumatisation is thus greater than that of adults because it disturbs the child's developmental process. The effect is often a repression or internalisation of memories that come to haunt the survivor in later life. The popular belief that children have no memory of their earliest experiences is false. In other words, a child is never too young to remember. Even infants store memory in sensory form, which sometimes causes painful flashbacks in adulthood. Sensory or auditory stimuli often produce these responses, including nightmares and flashbacks without clear context.

The pervasiveness of torture and abuse of children in many parts of the world reaches beyond any other kind of trauma experienced by human beings. In addition to witnessing the massive suffering of their parents and community, in some cases resulting in extreme loss, children experience constant fear. To survive such atrocity, they are compelled to abandon their childhood, become hyper vigilant, observant, analytical, and imaginative, since further torture and violence against themselves or their loved ones often remains imminent. We hear so many times at the RTC that parents could disappear suddenly. In some cases, children tell us how they could find themselves in a different hiding place every night. These types of stresses, irregularities and fears of what may happen, in addition to what has already transpired, interferes with a child's developmental phases and normal growth.

For any child in such a situation, survival means a suppression of any strong emotional response and dissociation of the reality around them. In some cases, crying silently or a plea of hunger and pain, could compromise the child's safety. Children thus learn to disable their feelings, facing torture and death in an unusually callous and apathetic manner. Although perhaps considered from an external perspective to be an unnatural child behaviour, professionals working with children who have endured the multiple and extreme stressors of war and persecution, will identify this behaviour as all too common and in many ways a predictable coping mechanism.

Repressing traumatic memories can lead a tortured child to constantly recreate the victim/perpetuator scenario in their mind around any social situation. If this tendency remains unattended, they may, in their adulthood, act it out with their own children, straining the parent/child relationship, causing recursive generational trauma. Other tortured children carry a constant and extreme sense of guilt or anxiety, usually because they do not understand why they survived when so many others died. It seems to them as if they, too, should have been killed.

For a tortured child, post-traumas are almost as great as the time of torture itself and its associated stresses. Often a consequence of an environment within which a child has been tortured is a full separation from loved ones, familiar cultural traditions and general way of life. Some children, fleeing violence and persecution are brought to live with strangers and accept them as their caretakers; some are later able to return to biological parents, but for many they are never able to see their families again. Those who become reunited with family after a long period may have the experience that so much time has passed; the biological family now feel like strangers to the child. After arrival to a safe location, some children are put into group homes and become wards of the host state—often placed into environments with children from other countries, with no common language or cultural knowledge. These children are expected to adapt—which many are remarkably capable of—but in the process, their past trauma and pain is often left unattended, in certain cases resulting in detrimental circumstances later in adult life.

Many of the children of refugees I have worked with would tell me that they didn't know what had happened to them and what was happening to them now; in a sense they could not find the vocabulary. They would describe that there was no possible way they could remember what happened, or that they didn't want to remember as they know somewhere in the back of their mind that they could not deal with the pain of remembering the atrocities endured. Some also came to believe that their memories were inaccurate or invalid, growing up with the belief they were unwanted and their parents were uncaring.

An issue that we should take into consideration is that despite the trauma a child may have faced, they will not cease being a child. Despite many large-scale human perpetrated atrocities, children have the capacity to play. Even in ghettos and concentration camps, where their games often took on disturbing and morbid characteristics of war, torture, and fights, they were able to cope in the ways they knew how, according to their level of resiliency and their development. Even those who developed bed-wetting and nightmares, are able to become social, make friends, and build attachments with their peers and adults around them with a little help. Through relating to others and building new attachments to their social workers, foster carers or supportive teachers at school, when family members are no longer present, a child develops a sense of happiness and connectedness again. Initially, of course, this is often difficult for many children, especially those without English language, since it is contrary to the previous culture. However, if social connection can happen in the host country, it allows a child to join groups and realise he or she is neither alone nor inferior—and start functioning socially without fear. Through these social links, children who are coping with traumatic memory and loss are able to regain some sense of self. In the course of realising their potential, they develop more psychic space and can find a sense of resilience, pride and purpose that ultimately can prevent the child from engaging with situations which may create further trauma and tragedy.

Once trust has been developed and they are psychologically strong enough, children who have been tortured make clear that healing their wounds brought on by trauma is made possible through talking to others and thinking about their experience, their loved ones and community. In our work with children who cannot verbalise their experiences, we use drawing, play and diary writing. Writing memoirs in a therapeutic, holding and supporting environment can be helpful because children can feel safe and ensured that the world will not forget what has been done to them—yet simultaneously feel confident that their story will not be shared unless they themselves choose to share it. In other words, the therapeutic space provides the possibility for a child to tell their story in whatever medium makes sense for them while also controlling who receives this information, as the space itself is guaranteed to be confidential unless there is risk of danger to the child or others. At the RTC, we have created groups with the hope of providing a forum to validate memories and identities, and develop a sense of belonging and hope. While some children find more comfort working one to one with a therapist, others may find even more security with their peers— others who have also experienced similar loss, grief and the struggle of resettlement.

Although we would never deny that children are made sufferers or wounded of war and rendered tragically vulnerable by exposure to senseless violence and resulting loss, we also firmly understand children to be resilient even in the face of extreme adversity. To foster the space for a traumatised child's resilience to grow, we have developed an approach that focuses on their capacity for resiliency, however small it may initially appear. We refer to this approach as a resilience-based therapeutic model. This approach recognises children's vulnerability while focusing on how a child can gain resilience in order to deal with memory of extreme trauma through having a listening other within therapeutic space. In our experience, through residence-focused inter-cultural therapy, children are able to gradually reach a productive and successful life with a positive identity—reiterating the importance of appropriate psychological support for youngsters who experienced unimaginable torture and human right violations.

Poverty and discrimination act as major barriers to the education for any child, yet the experience of the refugee child often includes significant levels of both. It is a nearly universal position, at least in rhetoric, that all children should enjoy the right to education regard-less of socio-economic status, cultural identity, sexuality, creed, or eth-nicity. To take advantage of this right, we can easily recognise that the protection of certain other rights must also be in place. In other words, if a child faces harassment from peers or authorities within the school sys-tem, or if a child is not properly nourished with food at home or during the day, this child will meet with exceeding difficulties when engaging with academic curricula as well as the social capital developed through an educational environment.

For many children of refugees, when education is provided the quality is often poor, and discrimination, particularly due to language and cul-tural differences, can significantly affect their educational experience. Due to the transitory situation children of asylum seekers may face, there are additional challenges that inhibit the child's ability to engage fully with the educational environment and thus, keep pace with their peers. Depending on issues of status, living conditions, economic resources of the family, etc., children may not be permitted to go to school or struggle to find their place and drop out. Refugee parents may find it challenging to support their children's schooling as they are unable to learn the edu-cation system in the UK due to lack of English language, or in part due to the under-resourced asylum support system.

A refugee parent's acquisition of the language of the host county can have a significant impact on the academic success of their children. Naturally, a child's capacity to learn the language used in their academic setting is fundamental to their achievement. However, if the parents do not learn or engage with the host-country language, this can act as a major barrier for the child. The vast majority of children speak their native language at home, but UK schools are taught in English and chil-dren are given no assistance to learn in a new language when they begin school at the age of five or six. Initially, a teacher may not be aware that a child speaks a different language at home, and even once they become aware of this, they will rarely speak the child's mother tongue. This will create a communication barrier not only between the teacher and child but also between the teacher and the child's parents. When children are unable to communicate with their teachers, they are at a distinct disadvantage that will place them behind their peers. Indeed, children who struggle with language are thought to be less likely to stay in school when they reach adolescence. Lack of education in the fundamental years harms the long-term prospects of refugee and asylum seekers' children, increasing the probability of poverty, restricted livelihood, and lack of appropriate social skills, and of course a potential risk of radicalisation as the young person needs attachment within peers. If he or she cannot maintain this need at school, the search for a place to belong can lead the young person to join a dangerous group. So, logically, a child's—and family's—capacity to learn the language of the host country can be an extremely influential factor on the rest of their lives.

On the contrary, children who stay in education and learn the English language very fast frequently become the main family interpreter, both within schools and in other institutional arenas, including the asylum system. The fact that they are children and their level of language corresponds to their age group, indeed often lacking the vocabulary used to report torture, persecutions, and other political issues, is forgotten, or better to say, neglected, both by parents and professionals who use them as a means to an end. In other words, the child is used as the cultural medium and interpreter which indirectly results in neglect and, in some cases, abuse. Many factors contribute to children taking on responsibility for their parents, including parents' inability to speak and to find work, economic insecurity, housing, and other welfare issues. A child exposed to this kind of family dynamic leaves little time for school work and as they grow older as more responsibility steadily gets pushed upon them.

Due to heightened levels of poverty commonly experienced in refugee families, parents may encourage children to take on many forms of labour, including working on the streets, shops or supermarkets at an early age to bring in additional, and occasionally the sole, income. This may further provoke the consequences of poverty on a child's educational attainment and future prospects, giving rise to a set of problems in accessing the most basic levels of service. In this way, the reasons for a child's poor attendance are directly related to the family's poverty, exclusion, and marginalisation. Parents may not send their children to school in order to minimise expenses, or they may choose which children to send (i.e., girls may be kept at home to do the household chores as well as to help the parents as an interpreter for GPs, hospital and welfare service visits). If a child can make a contribution to the family income through labour, that child may be unable to attend to school work or unable to meet scholastic success, despite high levels of intelligence. In sum, the danger inherent in a child's inability to attend school takes its toll over time and can lead to a persistent cycle of inter-generational poverty.

Even when children are able to attend school, poverty still affects their quality of education due to problems with associated costs of school, lack of suitable study spaces at home, and overcrowded households as well as overcrowded classrooms. Education can be the key to escaping the generational transfer of trauma and poverty, acting as an important resource for the development of resiliency.

It is important to recognise that schools in areas populated by refugee and asylum seekers children, by and large are overcrowded and understaffed. Indeed, there is often a lack of trained personnel and insufficient infrastructure, especially within inner-city London and the south-east boroughs. The government's budgeted expenditure and resources are too often limited with regard to keeping children in school and providing them with the support they need. Some children of refugee and asylum seekers may have not been in school prior to their arrival in the UK, either because schools were closed due to war or internal conflicts, or due to poverty and insufficient infrastructure.

Poverty and discrimination, often affecting children of refugees, families, and communities, persist as substantial barriers to the enjoyment of the right to education. Children of refugees are not provided support programmes to assist in making up for this gap. While school is mandatory for certain ages, the government does little to ensure that children regularly attend. Children may be enrolled to meet the legal requirements, but then may quickly drop out. Due to limitation of resources and capacity, administrators, and teachers may not be able to follow up with individual situations. It is important to note, within this context, that migration to London in recent decades also has led to a high rate of urban poverty and stretched capacity of local schools, having an impact on all children in those areas as well. High quality educational opportunities are lacking; the quality of educational instruction within these areas is substandard and the number of children per classroom is exceedingly high. These aspects, among others, demonstrate the significant variations in the quality of education delivered in different boroughs of London, with wealthier boroughs outperforming those with larger impoverished populations, populations which, whether refugee or not, receive inferior services.

Beyond merely educational discrimination, other significant inequalities affect the process of resettlement as well as the opportunity for refugee and asylum-seeking children to experience psychological wellbeing. Refugee and asylum-seeking children may arrive traumatised and disorientated, separated from their families, forced by persecution to leave their own countries and flee to the UK in search of safety. In the early developmental process, appropriate provision of support is extremely important in helping children of refugees and their carers while they rebuild their lives in the UK. From the experience of working with refugee and asylum-seeking families, and hearing their narratives, equal access is a serious impediment to many individuals and families integrating successfully and finding the support they need.

Such an inequality can be addressed through therapeutic intervention in order to help equalise the provision of vital services, and help those to use the Local Authority provisions effectively. It is known that asylum seeker and refugee families often have multiple and complex social needs, experience poverty, benefits restrictions and poor quality of temporary accommodation, all of which have a major impact on children and their carers. Some asylum seekers and children of refugees, young people and their families may also have special healthcare needs, which may include specific psychological needs. Children of refugees and young people, and especially their carers, may have particular linguistic needs before learning English. Often parents are keen for their children to be able to maintain and develop their home languages. The majority of those we serve are asylum seekers who speak very little or no English, many of whom are mothers or carers. This type of dilemma in asylum seeker or refugee families positions them as increasingly disadvantaged and socially excluded within this country.

Given the vastness of London, the cases where refugee or asylum seeker children are displaced from schools, nurseries, GP provision, neighbours, and friends are quite common. Children are passed around from one Local Authority to another, and some families report that they find it really difficult to obtain support under the Children Act 2004 and to be able to settle. Despite their great need, many asylum seeker and refugee families do not have access to the range of services that the general population does. This is due to a variety of reasons that may be complex and overlap, including lack of knowledge, no access to information about services in this country readily available in their own language, as well as frequent movements due to homelessness or temporary accommodation. In many cultures, there is significant unease or fear around leaving very young children with carers who do not speak the language the children speak at home, in addition to the possibility of racial harassment. Unfortunately, the unwelcome experience refugees may feel is quite widespread and has a direct impact on their feeling secure and connected to the services they may be involved in. This can result in lack of engagement. It is especially difficult when they are asked how much they can reveal about what was done to them. This is due to what they have experienced—a type of experience that goes to their heart and can block the child and young person's capacity to relate to others without fear. The combination of fear and mistrust of course can be, in part, the outcome of torture and repression people have endured in their home country. Those feelings and problems can gradually be addressed in a therapeutic relationship. But the child needs time to trust us and to understand what our position in their world model is. These processes of gaining trust in the therapeutic relationship also very much depends on their past and present experiences of other health and social care professionals and of people in positions of authority.

A child may have a different concept of fear than an adult, and parents may not share their fearful experiences or explain dangerous situations with their children. Children may be separated from their parents and other family members and be sent to safety by a parent or other family member before having experienced torture or other ill-treatment. This by and large happens without children's prior knowledge or understanding of why they were being sent away. This of course causes separation anxiety which can lead to depression and anxiety for children, but it is not related to the fears. Children may also be too young to comprehend what constitutes a risk and may not have awareness of fear and the reasons for it. A child's individual level of maturity and understanding is varied due to their age, as well as the environment and the process of development. Therefore the child may have difficulties articulating their fear in an interview with officials for their asylum application. It would help if the case workers look at sources of information available about the child's country of origin in order to inspect and scrutinise the child's immigration application. Refugee community organisations usually have the up-to-date information about their countries and can be helpful. Sometimes teachers and social workers also gain a lot of information about the country of origin from the child they are teaching or caring for, and can provide relevant and valid information specific to the child as well as refer to objective country information.

The fact is that a child cannot produce clear and objective evidence to support their asylum claim, and may find it difficult to describe details non-essential for them and to their direct experience, such as names, dates, places, persons, or organisations. So, considering the objective evidence in support of a child's case needs clear and an up-to-date relevant country of origin information.

Generally speaking, forms of persecution directly inflicted on children and adolescents are influenced by their age and physical ability amongst other factors. The range of child abuse includes forcible recruitment into military service, family or domestic violence, forced marriages of underage girls, discrimination against street children, female genital mutilation, forced labour, sexual exploitations, and forced prostitution, child pornography, trafficking, and children born outside of strict family planning laws and policies.

In such circumstances, the initial focus of a child is on safety and trust. So, trust is important and it is the primary need for the child. More work is required in adaptation to the trauma before recovery can be said to have occurred and reintegration can be achieved. The development of trust is an essential component in any form of engagement with a child. The person talking to the child should be encouraging, patient and empathic, but also permit time for the child to think and express their feelings the way they can.

The therapist may need to be prepared to declare an open commitment to supporting human rights issues in general, while remaining objective with regard to the therapeutic relationship. This commitment may need to be made explicit for a child or young person to create a reasonable trust within the therapeutic relationship. For therapists working in a country of repression, this often places them at considerable personal risk (Cienfuegos & Monelli, 1983). It is also important that therapists have an understanding of the cultural background from which their patient comes. This includes knowledge of the social and political context of the country of origin that the young person is coming from, which will provide the unique meaning that the torture and persecution has for the person, and what the particular experience symbolises for that person. Therefore, the therapeutic intervention should adopt an intercultural approach, taking into consideration the race, ethnic and the cultural outlook and expectations of the young person.

The fear response, prompted by reminders of the previous or primary trauma, may be an enduring reaction to persecution, brutalisation and torture the young person sustained. Methods that tend to lead to conditioning or adjustment of this response could be used within the therapeutic encounter for the young person's psychological recovery, and to prevent the development of post-traumatic stress.

There are considerable barriers to accessing health care, and specifically specialist mental health services, for refugee and ethnic minorities in general and indeed for young people. This is for numerous reasons, including language barriers, the lack of knowledge of available services and the fear or hostility of some health professionals in the host country based on the past experiences. In the UK, the lingering extended fear of not being accepted or being returned in the prolonged process of the asylum seeking, and the fact that often immigration cases and care of the child passes through various social workers, various foster carers, and also various levels of adjudication, are the biggest obstacles and barriers to appropriate treatment. The process of initial decision-making is, sadly, often rather unskilful and complex, and even for those young people whose cases are accepted there are long delays, which creates concerns for the young person.

CHAPTER EIGHT

Socio-psychological factors and institutional support

This chapter will address socio-psychological factors and the influence of institutional support or opposition for refugee and asylum seekers. As it is discussed throughout the book, refugee and asylum seeker children may arrive traumatised and disorientated separated from their families, forced by persecution to leave their own countries and come to the UK. In the developmental process, appropriate support provision is extremely important in helping children of refugees and their carers while they are rebuilding their lives in the UK. Sadly, refugee families in Britain do not have equal access to the existing range of services and interventions, even though their need for such provision may be greater, proportional to the general population. Through the narratives shared by refugee and asylum seeker families, and our witnessing this experience during therapeutic intervention, we can recognise this inequality.

Some asylum seekers and children of refugees, young people and their families may also have special healthcare needs, specifically psychological needs, which must be addressed in order to prevent future serious mental health problems. Children of refugees and young people and in some case their parents or family members as their carers, have particular linguistic needs before they are able to take advantage of necessary services. With more under-fives than in the general population in some refugee communities (our statistics indicate the Somali and Afghan families), they may have a greater need for a new dimension of mental health, and psychosocial intervention and education. In such circumstances adult refugee parents are amongst the most vulnerable and are unlikely to take part in any education and go through the process of adaptation and resettlement. Indeed, suffering psychologically and not being able to cope can cause tremendous tension between different generations within the family. This is particularly true for many refugee mothers who have responsibility for their children after having lost their informal support networks and extended families, which itself can lead to stress and psychological difficulties.

Experiences of exile often mean that family units and community networks are broken apart. In the case of refugee and asylum-seeking women particularly, this plays a huge role in their ability to care for their children and settle quickly. The unfamiliarity of the new culture is enough by itself to create significant disorientation; however, the isolation and lack of support resulting from the refugee experience can cause extreme depression and anxiety, sometimes regretfully inciting abusive or violent behaviour towards their children either verbally or physically, increasing the psychological problems for the children.

In London, particularly, the situation of isolation can be severe while people are awaiting a decision on their asylum application, as they may move around to temporary accommodation due to a lack of long-term resources provided through NASS and social services. Therefore, families with children who have already been uprooted on the journey to the UK, again have to go through painful and in some cases traumatic experiences of separation and loss from schools, nurseries, neighbours, and friends as they are passed around from one Local Authority to another. Some families reported that they find it really difficult to obtain support under the Children's Act, and as a consequence, find themselves unable to navigate the resettlement process.

A disproportionate number of refugee households are headed by women. There are many lone mothers in refugee communities because so many men have been killed in fighting or have been imprisoned while the mother was able to escape with the children. We hear specifically from asylum-seeking refugee families that, although they may identify their own needs readily, they are not aware of their social rights or services available to them within their host environment. The lack of knowledge they feel is frustrating and disempowering, leading many to have strong feelings that their needs have not been identified or met.

In general asylum seekers speak very little or no English. This dilemma puts asylum seeker and refugee families in a challenging position whereby they become subject to extreme social exclusion and their children similarly become some of the most socially marginalised children in the country.

Many asylum seeker and young refugee families face multiple social problems including difficulties in making an asylum application, finding a proper solicitor, living in poor housing, experiencing poverty as well as difficulties accessing services and receiving benefits. Some parents we serve feel that their social difficulties prevent them from being good parents. Specifically, depression amongst mothers, caused by social distress and isolation, was reported due to increased worry for their children as they are not able to be emotionally there for them. These isolated mothers feel very uncomfortable leaving their young children with child-minders or in the nursery from outside their community, especially in a community where no one speaks their home language. The majority of parents we see are usually unaware of the low cost or free services available for young children, such as libraries or toy libraries, or play groups or play sessions in community centres, sport centres or schools. Often they are not even aware of the after school clubs or homework clubs for older children at school.

The Local Authorities do not usually have clear inter-departmental planning and coordination for services for refugee and asylum seeker children and families. Refugee communities and organisations also have very little resources to provide provision for young children, as the refugee and asylum seeker families have multidimensional needs. Such families may be expecting national childcare agencies or services to provide for or tailor to refugees' needs; however this is almost always not the case.

This lack of knowledge, and thus inaccessibility of services, highlights the lack of early psycho-social intervention available for asylum-seeking young families. Some parents who reported not being able to cope or being violent physically or verbally are quite worried about their parenting skills and that is why they ask for help from us.

They are also extremely worried about how social workers and social services, as well as teachers, perceive their parenting skills. Some parents pointed to the cultural differences regarding physical punishment and their understanding of this form of punishment as being for the sake of the child in order to discipline them. Many parents are very concerned when child protection issues are raised with them and propose to get help and a proper assessment. They express a great amount of fear that social workers will accuse them of physical abuse or neglect and take their children away. Therefore they require great support and encouragement to be able to use resources from social services available to them when they are not able to cope.

One common fear amongst almost all different cultural backgrounds is separation from their children and lack of trust. Some asylum-seeking families are able to get in touch with refugee community organisations, but they may not live close enough to these organisations to get the support they need. Some asylum seekers and refugees do not wish to contact their community organisations which they do not know personally and therefore feel they cannot trust. Some female clients indicate that community organisations can be very much male dominated and it is quite unlikely they would get involved in the women's needs or issues, such as child care, domestic violence or a woman's wish to improve her English language.

Critical issues to the welfare of children of refugees and unaccompanied minors

The pain suffered by children throughout the world who are exposed to physical, mental, and emotional abuse and torture is immeasurable. In some countries, children have been tortured as part of collective punishments for whole communities, or as a means of extracting information from parents and/or their peers. Other children are tortured as a way of punishing and torturing their parents. In many countries around the world children are as likely as adults to be captured, imprisoned, and tortured. Therefore the treatment of child prisoners is a matter of increasing concern—particularly in some Asian, Latin American, and African countries such as Democratic Republic of Congo or Rwanda where, for the first time in history, children have been imprisoned and have to face trial for genocide.

We are far from a world without human rights abuses, impunity, and torture. The experience of being the subject of torture is often a precursor to psychological distress and psychiatric illness for children. The pervading sense of not being wanted attacks the wellbeing and hope of a child, especially those young people who live with endemic poverty, sadness, loneliness, uncertainty, and helplessness. Sometimes relatives or guardians are unable or psychologically incapable of caring for children within the context of conflict or civil unrest, while others are simply cruel and abusive directly to their child. In other cases, the parents or previous guardians may no longer be living, or are imprisoned, and thus their children are forced to stay with friends, community members or merely fend for themselves.

Children of refugees suffer from war and other forms of persecution in their countries of origin. Yet refugee and migrant children continue to suffer human rights abuses in countries of asylum, especially if they are separated from parents and caregivers. In the United States, Europe, and some other western countries, immigration services continue to detain significant numbers of children, unaccompanied and with their parents. In the United States, unaccompanied children are sometimes held in cells with juvenile offenders.

Below I bring an example of a child called Edwin, reported in the document published by Amnesty International entitled: "United States of America Unaccompanied Children in Immigration Detention" (2003). This vividly illustrates how injustice can easily be perpetrated at the level of the state against refugee and migrant children.

Edwin from Honduras was abandoned by his mother and lost his father in early childhood when he was only four years old and as the result he ended up living with a cousin who abused him, forcing him to work in the streets for money. He reported that: "When I didn't earn enough money, he punished me, beating me with a noose, car tools, and other objects, leaving scars on my body."

Edwin was afraid to go to the authorities because his cousin threatened to throw him out of house onto the street, and told him police would not protect a child like him. He was also afraid of living on the streets because he had heard that the authorities and gangs kill children living in the streets. When he was thirteen, he managed to leave for the US He said: "I had heard wonderful things about the US and how children were better treated here." He says he walked, begged, and worked for food to get to the US upon crossing the border he was arrested and detained. He was housed at the San Diego Juvenile Hall for almost six months, and he reports that he was mistreated by both guards and juvenile offenders.

> The officers did not know why I or other children picked up by the INS were there. They treated us the same as the others, as criminals. They were mean and aggressive and used a lot of bad words. […] Many of the other boys were violent, frequently looking for a fight. (2003)

He said that he was transported in full shackles during transfers and trips to court. He reports that after winning his asylum case, he left the jail for the last time, to be taken to a foster family. Again, he was transported in shackles. When he asked the INS officer why he needed shackles, he was told that it was to prevent his escape. He challenged the fact that he might try to escape since he had won his asylum. The officer allegedly responded that asylum is "just a piece of paper we can rip up, put you in jail and send you back to your country". Edwin was held in detention for eight months before being released. Edwin Larios Muñoz, testimony before the US Senate Committee on the Judiciary, Subcommittee on Immigration, 28th February 2002.

There are so many examples such as the above here in the UK. Asylum seekers and refugees referred to organisations such as the RTC by and large are young, single, or single parents. More than sixty per cent of people are under twenty-five years old. The top five countries of origin that during recent years children and young people are coming from includes Turkey, Somalia, Ethiopia, Eritrea, Iran, and Iraq. The majority of families are living in temporary accommodation. Some families are homeless, in some cases for more than two years. The times of being homeless by and large are on their arrival, or after they refuse NASS dispersal, and decide to stay in London or after leaving a detention centre. Mothers with young children have been held in detention centres in the UK. The availability of social support is limited. There are young adolescents who are living with siblings under eighteen years of age. More than eighty-five per cent of these children did not have a member of family or someone from their community and therefore have no social network or someone they can relate to when needed, and of course no facility or resources to contact anyone in their country of origin. The majority of children are coming from countries where there is ongoing conflict. Many experienced imprisonment, torture, and/or sexual and physical violence. Witnessing violence against their family or other members of their community is also a frequent experience, especially with unaccompanied minors that reported the death of parent/s or a family member due to violence. Many were involuntarily separated from members of their immediate family, and did not know their current whereabouts.

Many of the young adolescents and child refugees with whom I have worked in London report poor or inadequate support from social services, problems accessing health services and education, and serious concerns about being separated from their foster carer and being dispersed outside London when they are aged eighteen, and indeed, the fear of their immigration application being rejected. These young peoples' lives can further be confused and enmeshed with other issues such as age related disputes and detention. Those understandably exacerbate anxiety levels and other psychological consequences of torture that children and young people have already endured.

According to Home Office Statistics (GOV.UK) the number of children and adolescents seeking asylum in the UK is rising. Home Office Statistics show that one in four of those seeking asylum are children. Regardless of immigration rules, administrative status, socio-economic position, country of origin or skin colour these vulnerable young people seeking safety need protection and support. The 1989 UN Convention on the Rights of the Child created and built up the groundwork for protection of children and from it further legal provisions to protect children have emerged. Despite existing legislation internationally and nationally, there are serious shortcomings in the protection of children of refugees. It seems that these shortcomings are largely down to lack of resources together with poor management and a shortage of systematic research about key issues.

Defective interpretations of the rule of law, or generalisation and conceptualisation of refugees' experience, in particular children, apart from political and economic influences, are due to inadequate empirical data and knowledge. These leads to dangerous and in some cases life-threatening shortcomings in the protection of children of refugees (please see the Mrs G & her baby case from Westminster in London). A major contributing factor to these shortcomings can be the influenced mainly on lack of resources, specifically the financial resources for health and social care and most recent year massive cut in the name of austerity. Another important factor is the use of western psychological models which bring a lack of understanding about cultures and social contexts that these children come from. Effective policy requires sound theories and sound empirical data, not assumptions underlying western conventional practice. I maintain that the dominant idea of childhood as a universalised and paradoxically much individualised construct that is built on notions of vulnerability and incompetence has led to interventions that unintentionally undermine children's resilience and denigrate their capacity.

It is a well-known fact that children of refugees have been exposed to various stressors. They are exposed to stressors in their country of origin (which are often the reason they must flee), during their flight and travel to safety which usually can be extremely difficult and by and large involve further abuse and violence; indeed the uncertainty and anxiety during their asylum application a process that may takes considerable lengths of time. The asylum-seeking process after the age of eighteen involves bureaucratic hurdles that can re-traumatises the young person and of course the process of settlement and integration after the immigration matter resolved and the young person have full refugee states. The young person will have to work with a range of social, cultural, and economic barriers and vastly learn how to interact with the system while carrying with their education and in many cases learning to leave alone or sharing accommodation with strangers.

For some children, fleeing to safety often means leaving their homes without any knowledge, sometimes without parents telling them anything, without goodbye or personal belongings. They often do not have any cultural awareness of the environment to which they are going to and that they must overcome the hurdles of adapting to a new language and a new culture. During the process of settlement in the new country, refugee families are commonly live in deprived neighbourhoods with high levels of crime due to minimal economic and social power. In their daily lives, they often suffer from acute discrimination, particularly as a result of the increased implementation of "dispersal" policies whereby they are distributed into more rural and poor communities throughout the country. So, the challenges of integration for such children and their families are multi-layered. Moreover, unattended psychological symptoms resulted from previous traumatic experiences add tremendous difficulties for children in the process of settlements.

Children's experiences of war, torture, persecution, and the flight from home countries can lead to a sense of constant fear. It is important to note that apart from the risks that all children and adolescents experience, refugee children who have been tortured or persecuted have the added stress of having to live with distant relatives or foster families whilst taking on adult responsibilities. This can lead to problems with young refugees' identities and educational attainment, influencing gaps in inter-generational understanding, deterioration of family cohesion and possible delinquency, neglect and abuse which ultimately add to community strain.

Many children of refugees, although living in the west, may find themselves in difficult situations that undermine their opportunities to grow up as happy, healthy, educated, and responsible members of the community in which they live. Those that succeed are a tribute to their resilience, and early healthy psychological development that provide potential to adapt.

The cultural issues impacting children of refugees can stem from a family's understanding of the therapeutic process. First there can be confusion over the parent's *vs.* an institution's assessment of a child's mental health. Following this, the family's demands and the cultural values can also be threatened by the interview process. Language difficulties often place pressure on younger generations to mediate public interactions, particularly with officials or when acquiring services. This situation becomes especially harmful when a child is used as an interpreter by parents and professionals allow it to continue without question. A child used as an interpreter or intermediary between professionals and their parents can detrimentally affect or distort the child's mental health.

Psychological intervention can play an important role in meeting the needs of refugees and asylum seekers, their children and families, by combating the social exclusion of this population, as well as preventing further stress, further anger, and further acting out. Some parents express concern that their children are losing the language and culture of their own home country. They also worry that their children will grow up with very different values to their own and may become alienated from their parents as a result. There is some evidence that supports this fear, as the younger generation of children learn English very quickly in comparison to their parents and often become more quickly adapted to the cultural norms of the host country.

Some refugee and asylum seeker parents use their young children as interpreters and translators without recognising that their English understanding is quite similar to their own, and that the experience of acting as intermediary itself can create further trauma to children and young people. As discussed before, with more under-fives and young people than in the general population, refugees and asylum seekers may have a greater need for earlier provision of service. This in itself puts the children in an unequal position to the general or indigenous population. The lack of training and courses on refugee's issues, language, working with interpreters, and anti-discriminatory practice, prevents professionals from meeting the children of refugees' healthcare and emotional needs, and it prevents these children and families from using healthcare professionals within the community during the early years.

Children who have experienced torture

The United Nations Convention Against Torture in Article 1 defines torture as:

> Any act by which severe pain or suffering, whether physical or mental, is intentionally inflicted on a person for such purposes as obtaining from him or a third person information or a confession, punishing him for an act he or a third person has committed or is suspected of having committed, or intimidating or coercing him or a third person, or for any reason based on discrimination of any kind, when such pain or suffering is inflicted by or at the instigation of or with the consent or acquiescence of a public official or other person acting in an official capacity. It does not include pain or suffering arising only from, inherent in or incidental to lawful sanctions. (Audiovisual Library of International Law, UN Convention against Torture, and other Cruel, Inhumane or Degrading Treatment or Punishment, Article 1, Paragraph 1)

Article 3 of the European Convention on Human Rights (1950a) states that that: "No one shall be subjected to torture or to inhumane or degrading treatment or punishment." Article 3 is an absolute right prohibiting torture, and inhumane or degrading treatment or punishment. The state must not itself engage in torture, or in inhumane or degrading treatment. It is also obliged to prevent such treatment happening, and to carry out an investigation into allegations that it has. The state must comply with its obligations within its territory and, in exceptional circumstances, in different countries where it exercises effective jurisdiction. The prohibition on torture has been part of the British common law framework since the eighteenth century. Today the legal framework around torture is considerably more sophisticated. It is prohibited both by civil law and by several Acts of Parliament. The UK has ratified several international conventions prohibiting torture and ill-treatment. This framework is supported by an institutional structure of regulators, including the Care Quality Commission (CQC), the Independent Police Complaints Commission (IPCC) and Her Majesty's Chief Inspectorate of Prisons for England and Wales (HMI Prisons) in line with the UN Convention Against Torture, Article 3, Equality and Human Rights Commission.

Three institutions are in place to protect individuals who are users of health and social care services. The Care Quality Commission (CQC) was established in 2009 to regulate, register, inspect, and review health and adult social care services in the public, private, and voluntary sectors in England. The CQC can take legal action against providers that fail to meet the minimum requirements outlined by the CQC's essential standards.

Children who might be detained in young offender institutions or at the secure training centres or secure children's homes are under the full control of the Local Authorities, so the responsibilities of the state are heightened and augmented. Because of the vulnerability of young people in these circumstances the threshold of severity for defining torture, inhumane or degrading treatment or punishment is lessened.

Under Article 3, the state:

> [...] is required to have both laws and systems in place to prevent people suffering ill-treatment at the hands of other individuals. This means that criminal laws must be effective and punish those who perpetrate torture, and inhumane or degrading treatment. It also means that public authorities have an obligation to act to protect vulnerable individuals from ill-treatment that reaches the level of severity of Article 3, when they know or should have known about it. (*Human Rights Review*, 2012: 71)

- There is evidence that restraint is used extensively, but better data is needed;
- Authorised restraint techniques used in young offender institutions and secure training centres do not meet human rights standards;
- The use of restraint as a form of discipline, rather than in cases of absolute necessity or safety, is in breach of Article 3;
- Possible breaches of Article 3 in these settings are not always effectively investigated.

Freedom from torture and inhumane or degrading treatment or punishment is:

> An absolute right. This right applies even during a war or in times of threats to national security. States can never, under any circumstances, suspend or derogate from this article, be it for public order purposes or in the interest of society, or due to threats to national security. Everybody has a right to protection under Article 3, regardless of his or her identity or actions. (*Human Rights Review*, 2012:73)

Many tortured children have lived in circumstances that most of us could never imagine. The dynamic of sexual violence does not imply older perpetrators and younger victims, evident in disturbing incidents, such as the one in the Renamo camps in Mozambique, where young boys, who themselves had been traumatised by violence, frequently inflicted sexual violence on young girls (Mozambique ex-rebel Renamo camp, reported by the BBC on 8th March 2012). The layers and complexity of sexual violence against children cannot be ignored. However, this should not stand in the way of protecting against the profound and lasting damage caused by such acts. Even girls who are not forcibly raped may still be obliged to trade sexual favours for food, shelter or physical protection for themselves, their baby or younger siblings. In these cases as well, however, one could argue that such acts are also forced in this way as it becomes a matter of survival.

The rise of sexually transmitted diseases, particularly HIV/AIDS, for those pushed into sex work is a predictable consequence, creating further levels of stigmatisation as well as severe health impacts. In the case of Uganda, a common factor contributing to the high rates of AIDS was the sex trade that grew exponentially during the country's civil war when girls, in an effort to preserve their own security, were pushed into selling their bodies for protection. There are currently an estimated 1.2 million people living with HIV in Uganda, which includes 150,000 children; and an estimated 64,000 people died from AIDS in 2009 and 1.2 million children have been orphaned by Uganda's devastating epidemic (reports: 1.Government of Uganda (2010, March) "UNGASS country progress report: Uganda"; 2. UNAIDS (2010) "UNAIDS report on the global AIDS epidemic"). Due to inappropriate or insufficient treatment following such trauma, many young girls suffer the consequences of such torture to the end of their lives.

Tragically, child trafficking is increasingly developing into a fast growing industry with devastating human consequences. It is no longer a rare issue, or the case of those families trying to send their child to the UK for better future prospects. Instead, children are now brought into the country for sexual exploitation, as a servant or for other labour exploitation, involvement in drug dealing and other criminal activity. Although these children may not be involved directly in a war zone, or in a conflict environment, they are also often forced to endure much of the same treatment as those who are.

Abduction and trafficking of young girls for sale into prostitution and slavery is a serious problem that has existed for many centuries. Although international conventions and agreements have been raised to address and prohibit this tragic phenomenon, we see no less of it in the modern era. Desperation from poverty is a common cause of trafficking, but arguably no more so than the commodification of women and girls during war time, where they are reduced to "spoils" reaped from the enemy's lot. As physical brutality visited upon those egregiously traded in this way often leaves horrific visible and internal scarring for life, so, too, do the emotional and psychological consequences.

Children exploited for trafficking are generally those of families who are living in extreme poverty in the home country or under the threat of political conflict or civil war. The intention to create a better future somewhere else for one's children is often largely part of the motivation. However, desire for a better life with the promise of money, safety, and security is enough to entice some adolescents and young people to make the decision themselves. Trafficked children and young people whom we have served have shared that the people responsible for bringing them to the UK often take their passport and threatened them with violence and killing their family if they do not do what they are told.

So, many of these young people who have been trafficked and forced into prostitution and domestic slavery are disorientated and isolated, and have very low self-esteem and confidence, which often prevents them from positively effecting change in their lives. Indeed, they find it difficult to accept help or trust professionals offering help. When they can trust, they become quite dependent as they had been on their perpetuators, emotionally as well as physically. The lack of confidence and self-esteem which results in lack of psychic space and resiliency can result in aggressive and anti-social behaviour, restricting opportunity, and creating disruption in education.

What needs to be done (and what we are doing at the RTC through my work):

- Provide considerable care and engagement in a therapeutic space;
- Take confidentiality very seriously—beyond risk factors, do not share details;
- Multi-agency action at all levels with a good liaison;
- Law enforcement to redress the violation of the child within the UK and the child's home country if possible for retribution and justice;
- Implement the Children's Act (1989) and its amendment at all times for safeguarding the person, rather than focusing on criminalisation.

Article 17 of the European Social Charter, The Right of Mothers and Children to Social and Economic Protection (1961), indicates:

> With a view to ensuring the effective exercise of the right of mothers and children to social and economic protection, the Contracting Parties will take all appropriate and necessary measures to that end, including the establishment or maintenance of appropriate institutions or services.

In September 2000, the Committee on the Rights of the Child held the first of two General Discussion days on violence against children. It focused on "State violence to children" and following the day the Committee adopted detailed recommendations, including the prohibition of all corporal punishment. The Committee recommends that States parties should review all relevant legislation to ensure that all forms of violence against children, however light, are prohibited, including the use of torture, or cruel, inhuman or degrading treatment such as beating, whipping, corporal punishment or other violent measures for chastisement and retribution or disciplining within the child justice system, or in any other context. The Committee recommends that such legislation should ensure to include appropriate sanctions for violations and the provision of rehabilitation for injured party. The Committee urged the initiation of public information campaigns to raise awareness and inform the public about the gravity and seriousness of human rights violations and the harmful impact of these violations on children, and also to address cultural acceptance of violence against children, and promoting instead zero-tolerance of violence. The Committee encouraged non-governmental organisations to prepare and present evidence for public knowledge regarding torture and violence against children, including what might culturally perceived "acceptable" forms of violence against children.

The Committee on the Rights of the Child published its concluding observations on States examined at the 60th session (29th May–15th June 2012). The issue of corporal punishment was raised with all states, with recommendations to prohibit corporal punishment in all settings, including the home, made to Algeria, Australia, Turkey, and Vietnam. The Committee also recommended the repeal of legal defences for the use of corporal punishment, appropriate public education and awareness raising programmes, child participation in the development of preventive strategies, professional training, and research on the issue. The Committee welcomed the achievement of prohibition of all corporal punishment in Greece. To Cyprus, where corporal punishment is unlawful in all settings, the Committee recommended that law reform be completed by formal repeal of the defence in the Children Law.

Explicit prohibition in the home and other settings was recommended to Andorra, Bosnia and Herzegovina, Liberia, and Namibia. To Canada, the Committee expressed "grave concern" at section 43 of the Criminal Code which provides for the use of force "by way of correction" and at the Supreme Court's 2004 ruling which upheld the law, recommending that section 43 be repealed. The Committee welcomed prohibition in Albania and recommended effective implementation; Austria's measures to support implementation of prohibition were noted and recommendations made to strengthen and expand them.

Ratification of the Optional Protocol to the Convention on the Rights of the Child on a Communications Procedure has begun: it was ratified by Thailand and acceded to by Gabon in September 2012. It has been signed by 34 other states. The Committee on the Rights of the Child's comments and recommendations regarding corporal punishment were made following examination of States' reports from January 1993 to October 2012.

The Third Optional Protocol (OP3) to the Convention on the Rights of the Child (CRC) allows children or their representatives to report rights violations directly to the UN Committee on the Rights of the Child, which will then investigate their complaints, and can ask governments to take action. The International Coalition Ratify OP3 for the CRC is a coalition of nearly one hundred national, regional and international non-governmental organisations and networks, human rights institutions and other non-governmental bodies from around the world, committed to achieving universal ratification of the OP3.

The Special Representative of the UN Secretary-General on Violence against Children and the International Coalition Ratify OP3 on the CRC welcome the recent ratifications of Ireland, Monaco and Andorra during the Treaty Event on the occasion of the UN General Assembly. They are calling upon more governments to solidly commit to children's rights by ratifying the OP3 before the Convention's 25th anniversary on November 20th 2014. The OP3 entered into force in April 2014. Children can only submit a complaint to the UN Committee on the Rights of the Child if their national legal system has been unable to provide an effective solution. The UN Committee on the Rights of the Child will hear complaints against any country that has ratified the OP3. Fourteen countries: Albania, Andorra, Belgium, Bolivia, Costa Rica, Gabon, Germany, Ireland, Monaco, Montenegro, Portugal, Slovakia, Spain, and Thailand have ratified the OP3. An additional thirty-five countries have signed the OP3, showing their support and intention to ratify.

In 2014 Third Optional Protocol to the Convention on the Rights of the Child on a Communications Procedure, the International Coalition Ratify OP3CRC, together with the leading UN experts on children's rights, including Kirsten Sandberg, Chairperson of the Committee on the Rights of the Child, the Special Representatives of the Secretary-General for Children and Armed Conflict, Leila Zerrougui, and on Violence against Children, Marta Santos Pais, as well as the Special Rapporteur on the Sale of Children, Child Prostitution, and Child Pornography, Maud de Boer-Buquicchio, call on all States to make a quantum leap on the path to justice for children through the ratification of the Third Optional Protocol without delay.

These campaign developments are important for protecting children from exploitation and trafficking. Trafficking of children is a form of human trafficking for the purpose of exploitation that has been internationally recognised as a human rights violation. There are no appropriate and correct statistics about the magnitude of child trafficking, but the International Labour Organization (ILO) estimates that 1.2 million children are trafficked each year. Yet, it is only within the past decade that the prevalence and complications of this practice have risen only due to an increase in research and campaigns. A variety of potential solutions have accordingly been suggested and implemented, which can be categorised as four types of action: 1. broad protection; 2. prevention; 3. law enforcement; 4. assistance. Major international documents regarding child trafficking include the 1989 UN Convention on the Rights of the Child, the 1999 International Labour Organization, Worst Forms of Child Labour Convention, and the 2000 UN Protocol to Prevent, Suppress and Punish Trafficking in Persons, especially Women and Children. The Optional Protocol on the Sale of Children, Child Prostitution and Child Pornography is a protocol of the Convention on the Rights of the Child, formally adopted by the United Nations in 2000, which formally requires all states to prohibit the sale of children, child prostitution, and child pornography. According to the ILO, sexual exploitation of children includes all of the following:

- The use of girls and boys in sexual activities remunerated in cash or in kind (commonly known as child prostitution) in the streets or indoors, in such places as brothels, discotheques, massage parlours, bars, hotels, restaurants, etc.;
- The trafficking of girls and boys and adolescents for the sex trade;
- Child sex tourism;
- The production, promotion and distribution of pornography involving children;
- The use of children in sex shows (public or private).

Though measuring the extent of this practice is difficult due to the criminal and covert nature of the problem, the ILO estimates that there are as many as 1.8 million children sexually trafficked worldwide, while UNICEF's (2006) State of the World's Children Report reports this number to be 2 million.

An asylum-seeking child may be a trafficked child if they have been moved into a situation where they are exploited. Children may be trafficked for a variety of different reasons. There is considerable information on safeguarding a child who may have been trafficked including, "Every child matters and human trafficking" (2003); also "Working together to safeguard children" (HM Government, 2010), and "What to do if you suspect a child is being abused" (2006) and Arrangements to Safeguard and Promote the Welfare of Children for those Exercising UK Border Agency Functions. To get advice or gather more information the NSPCC can be contacted. National Child Trafficking Advice and Information telephone is 0800 107 7057, also the United Kingdom Human Trafficking Centre can be contacted on 0114 252 3891 or 0800 1800.

In having a regard to the need to safeguard and promote the welfare of children, case workers who may encounter children in the course of their work need to be sensitive to potential indicators that a child may have been trafficked, including:

- At port of entry the child may have entered the country illegally, either with no travel documents or on false documents;
- The child has a prepared story very similar to that which other children have given;
- The child is unable to confirm the name and address of the person meeting them on arrival;
- The child's journey or visa has been arranged by someone other than their family;
- The child is accompanied by an adult who insists on remaining with them at all times;
- The child may appear withdrawn and refuses to talk or appears fearful to a person in authority;
- The sponsor has previously made multiple visa applications for other children and/or has acted as the guarantor for other children's visa applications. They may have/or be known to have acted as the guarantor on the visa applications for other visitors who have not returned to their countries of origin on the expiry of those visas;
- A child currently residing in the UK goes missing from local authority care;
- A poor relationship exists between the child and their adult carers;
- The child may be one among a number of unrelated children found at the same address;
- The child is not enrolled or stopped attending school or is having irregular attendance.

In cases where a child appears to have been trafficked, an immediate referral needs to be made to the Local Authority social worker and or local police for the area in which the child is currently residing.

There are also issues that need to be taken into consideration to prevent potential risk of the child being re-trafficked and therefore the risk of future harm through exploitation and abuse. When encountering the child it is important to collect and draw together information about the child's family, community and general conditions in the country of origin before considering any major decision. The UNHCR have produced guidance on the application of Article 1A (2) of the 1951 Convention and/or 1967 Protocol relating to the Status of Refugees to victims of trafficking and persons at risk of being trafficked. The ILO has found that girls involved in other forms of child labour, such as domestic service or street vending, are also at the highest risk of being pulled into commercial child sex trafficking, and that the increased use and availability of the internet has served as a resource for traffickers, increasing the incidence of child sex trafficking. The exchange of sex for food, shelter, drugs/alcohol, money and/or approval by children is not a lifestyle choice—it is child abuse (Kingsley & Mark, 2001).

Looking at some statistics on the sexual exploitation of children and young people, the Stop Sex with Children website provided the below evidence:

- Approximately 400 children and young people are being sexually exploited on the streets of Winnipeg each year. (Statistics include only visible sex trade exploitation).
- 80% of child sexual exploitation is hidden in "gang houses" and "trick pads".
- Thirteen years old is the average age that children reported their first experience of being exploited through the sex trade. Age range is from 8 years to 16 years old.
- 70%–80% of adults involved in the sex trade were also first exploited under the age of 18.
- 85%–90% of sexually exploited children/young people are female; 10%–15% are male.
- 52% children were sexually exploited and 52% were physically abused as children.
- 81% were runaways.
- 33% were homeless.

- 72% were in the care of Child and Family Services.
- 93% had involvement with drugs and alcohol.
- 53% had used alcohol before the age of 12.
- Seven times is the average number of attempts individuals had made trying to escape or leave the sex trade.
- 44% have been treated for an emotional problem by a psychiatrist, psychologist, or counsellor.
- 38% have attempted suicide.
- 63% failed or repeated a grade in school. 77% were suspended from school.
- Average education level is grade 8.
- 70%–80% of children and youth exploited in Manitoba are of Aboriginal descent. (Source: www.stopsexwithkids.ca/app/en)

When working with children of refugees in a therapeutic setting, it is important to note that presenting problems should not be seen as totally different and separate from those of other children who may be unhappy and distressed. It is also important to be aware that children of refugees come from a wide range of cultures and have had very varied experiences. Therefore, they present their needs and difficulties in a variety of ways. There is no one recognisable pattern of behaviour. However, it is useful to think about some of the difficulties which some children of refugees have in common; such as past memory that continues to affect their daily life.

Understanding a child's distress before any intervention is begun is very important. Children who have been hurt and have lost so much are not going to start feeling safe quickly. We may not be able to actively engage them straight away, but we can help them cope with their feelings by providing respect and moving at the child's pace.

It is not acceptable to sit and watch the world the way it is and the way children are treated around the world without responding. We have to stand and say loudly and repeatedly that torturing children is wrong anywhere in this world. The abolishment of child torture, in all its forms, should become a priority for all human rights organisations and government policy. Work permits for the staff of international NGOs and access for some missions in the field, should only be provided to those who recognise the priority to protect children. Improvement of our monitoring systems for children's rights violations is an issue demanding immediate attention both at the local and international level. As we consider strategic allocation of funding to promote peace and long-term stability of specific regions, commissioning for such work should be at the forefront within both humanitarian and rehabilitation organisations.

As clinicians, we must affirm a commitment to protect the rights of children. Many children of refugees suffer appalling violence as soldiers, but even those who remain "civilians" can be subjected to horrific experiences. Children of refugees need to be helped to overcome the highly stressful experiences they have endured, and their views and perspectives need to be treated as a source of learning and strength, not weakness. We need to use children's negative experiences to create positive outcomes.

As well as the risks that all adolescents face, many refugee young people who have been tortured in particular have the added stresses of having to live with distant relatives or foster families and take on adult responsibilities. Combinations of these factors can lead to problems in the areas of:

- Personal and cultural identity;
- Educational attainment;
- Inter-generational misunderstanding;
- Lack of family cohesion, which may lead to delinquency, neglect, abuse, and community strain.

The challenges for young refugees are complex and often mutually enforcing. Their traumatic experience of war, torture, persecution, and flight from their native countries causes a sense of loss and a presence of constant fear.

This is specifically the case since the acceptance of the UN Convention on the Rights of the Child (1989). Despite this progressive Convention to further establish binding protection for children internationally, many shortcomings remain. A defective conceptualisation of refugees, in particular children, persists largely due to inadequate empirical data and knowledge. The issue of protection is made difficult by lack of resources, bringing with it poor management and the inability to develop systemic research about key issues.

Many services for children of refugees are led by stereotypical notions of social norms, values, dynamics, and power structures. In order to avoid these stereotypes there is a need to contextualise projects and to give greater attention to the ethnographic needs of children to ensure greater resiliency, and indeed, closer sociocultural adaptation for children of refugees and asylum seekers. This is to assure greater opportunity for developing capacity for resilience, sustainability and closer social and cultural adaptation for the people that we set ourselves to serve.

If children are to be helped to overcome the highly stressful experiences they have endured, their views and perspectives need to be treated as a source of learning and strength, not weakness. It is important to acknowledge the painful, humiliating, and profoundly debilitating experiences that many children of refugees suffer during periods of war, torture or other forms of political violence. Simultaneously, it has to be recognised that the dominant discourse of vulnerability, sickness, crisis, and loss has the potential for seriously undermining children's current wellbeing, although it may be what seems to characterise their prior experiences. The physiological experience of suffering undoubtedly has universal characteristics for human beings that have a limited repertoire of responses to catastrophic experiences. However, despite what similarities we may observe, different responses occur across cultures.

Therefore, in assisting children of refugees and young people who have been tortured, we, as campaigners and service providers need to have access to in-depth information about cultures, the nature of the trauma they have endured, family dynamics, and special needs. While recognising the limitations to verbal communication and the impact of trauma on recounting details of experience, it is essential to listen carefully to children. If we are to effectively respond to the need for appropriate intervention in cases of child torture and trauma, the inclusion of culturally and linguistically relevant teams in this process cannot be overlooked.

To provide the opportunity for children to develop resiliency and regain well-being in the aftermath of experiences of torture and violence perpetrated against them or their loved ones, intervention methods must be philosophically and anthropologically reoriented to adjust for cultural and linguistic differences as well as different phases in the child's life. Before the possibility exists for dealing with loss and pain at such a degree, productive partnerships between the child and the mental health professional need to be established. As the partnership is developed, the full scale of the impact of torture and traumatic previous experience often becomes increasingly apparent. Threats, and acts, of persecution, torture, and death are aimed at a complete destabilisation. The end result is often a complex experience of anxieties, creating a potentially dynamic and inconsistent presentation or one that might be expected from other forms of traumatic suffering.

Beyond the extreme trauma embedded in prior experience, refugees frequently experience on-going traumatic anxiety due to unresolved status once arriving in the host country. The corrosive experience of living in limbo in this way may impart devastating harm on one's own self-image and sense of permanence in the world. It results in a permanent sense of dislocation, not only from familiar domestic geography and culture which occurs from the flight onwards, but also within the resettlement process a persisting awareness of not belonging and exclusion. Existing invisibly without the external markers by which they know themselves and their worth leads to depression, various levels of identity crisis, as well as anger and aggression.

I identify the development of a framework for conceptualising the risk factors, from a clinical, social, and legal point of view, as a critical step toward creating stronger, more comprehensive approaches to respond to the complex needs of children who have endured torture and maltreatment. The fragility of the situation begs the need for a suitable framework from the clinical perspective. Informed by my professional experience, there are two important questions that require consideration in order to create such a guide: 1. If therapy is primarily aimed at gentle explorations of one's worst fears, then what purchase can it have on this most ungentle process of a tortured child? And 2. What is needed by those who have come finally to rest in some refuge to heal the wounds of external trauma, due to torture and their environmental impingement?

As we begin to address these questions thoroughly, several specific issues also induce consideration such as:

- The power of communications and the use of words in treating trauma that comes from physical and bodily privation that combined with psychological pressure;
- The identification of psychological strengths and weakness by which we can identify those whose resilience carry them through so far and start from there;
- The place of social network support and its loss.

CHAPTER NINE

Obstacles to monitoring and eradicating torture

The reality is that we are far from a world without human rights violations, impunity, and torture of children and adults. As professionals working to support children of refugees, several issues need to be kept in perspective:

- Refugees and asylum seeker children leave behind a home, at times becoming stateless and in many cases losing everything;
- They often have personally experienced or witnessed the rape and murder of loved ones;
- Some are forced to watch their homes razed to the ground;
- Some have suffered pain and physical damage at the hands of torturers;
- Some may have walked hundreds of miles seeking a place of safety or if they had any money to pay an agent to arrange a passage to safety;
- Many may come with scars both physical and psychological that run deep, often the wounds of the recent past re-stimulate the wounds from long past.

The Optional Protocol on the Involvement of Children in Armed Conflict is a protocol of the Convention on the Rights of the Child, formally adopted by the United Nations in 2000. Essentially, the protocol states that while volunteers below the age of eighteen can voluntarily join the armed forces, they cannot be conscripted. As the Protocol reads, "State parties shall take all feasible measures to ensure that member of their armed forces who have not attained the age of 18 years do not take a direct part in hostilities" (2000). Despite this, the ILO estimates that "tens of thousands" of girls and boys are currently forcibly enlisted in the armed forces in at least seventeen countries around the world. Children conscripted into the armed forces can then be used in three distinct ways.

On 13th September 2013 All Africa reported that more than 550 children in the Democratic Republic of the Congo (DRC) had left armed groups in the previous five months, according to the United Nations humanitarian relief arm. "The awareness campaign calling for children to leave armed groups succeeded in demobilising 557 children between March and August", the UN Office for the Coordination of Humanitarian Affairs (OCHA) said in a statement.

The children had been relocated from the territories of Malemba Nkulu, Manono, Mitwaba, and Pweto, in Katanga province. Some 444 children were in temporary centres in Kalemie, Lubumbashi, and Manono, while 113 others have been reunited with their families, OCHA said. An additional 1,500 children are still in the ranks of armed groups in the province, according to the UN Children's Fund (UNICEF, 2009) which supports the release campaign.

The Secretary-General's Special Representative for Children and Armed Conflict, Leila Zerrougui, has cautioned that thousands of children continue to be abducted, recruited, killed, maimed, or raped in conflicts around the world. The DRC has signed Action Plans to end the recruitment and use of children, as well as sexual violence against children (source: www.allafrica.com).

The assessment of a child's asylum application has to be in line with the requirements set out in the UN Convention Rights of the Child (UNCRC) and the duty under section 55 of the UK Borders, Citizenship and Immigration Act 2009, indeed the Protection of Children Act (1989). The need to safeguard and promote the welfare of children in the UK has to be the primary concern at all times in the process, with the same standard. A reasonable degree of the likelihood of a well-founded fear of persecution, amongst other matters should also be taken into account. A child should be given opportunity to discuss specific matters and any factors that may have impact on their livelihood. This will help the likelihood of misinterpretation of the child circumstances. Further, in assessing a child's application the framework set out at paragraphs 349 to 352 of the Immigration Rules and any other public commitments made on children should be taken into account, as well as factors that would affects a child's manner and behaviour such as age, education, maturity, gender, the standing of the child's family in the community, their life experience, history of trauma endured, the cultural expectations and characteristics traits expected of the children in their country of origin, and any other objective factors and information relating to the child's claim. The ability of a child to be able to clarify the situation if any discrepancies are observed and whether it is right to pursue the child for more information or clarification during the interview needs to be considered. If this is absolutely needed the individual interviewer or case worker always need to take into consideration the requirements of Article 3 of the UN Convention on the Rights of the Child.

Recent research conducted by the Coalition to Stop the Use of Child Soldiers has also noted that girl soldiers must be uniquely recognised, in that they are especially vulnerable to acts of sexual violence. The incidence of child soldiers has become especially relevant in popular culture following the Kony 2012 movement, which aimed to arrest Joseph Kony, a Ugandan war criminal who is responsible for the trafficking of thousands of child soldiers and sex slaves.

Children are also used in drug trades in all regions of the world. Specifically, children are often trafficked into exploitation as either drug couriers or dealers, and then "paid" in drugs, such that they become addicted and further entrapped. Due to the illicit nature of drug trafficking, children who are apprehended are often treated as criminals, when in reality they are often the ones in need of legal assistance. While comprehensive worldwide statistics regarding the prevalence of this practice are unknown, several useful regional studies have been conducted. For example, the International Organization for Migration (IOM) has recently investigated the use of Afghan children in the heroin trade and child involvement in the drug trades of Brazil.

Luke Dowdney (2013) who studied children in the drug trade in Rio de Janeiro, Brazil found that children involved in the drug trades are at significantly higher risk of engaging in violence, particularly murder.

Forced child begging is another child exploitation in which under-age boys and girls are forced to beg through psychological and physical coercion. Begging is defined by the *Buffalo Human Rights Law Review* as "the activity of asking for money as charity on the street". There is evidence to suggest that forced begging is one industry that children are trafficked into, with an UNICEF study (2010) reporting that thirteen per cent of trafficking victims in South Eastern Europe have been trafficked for the purpose of forced begging. The United Nations protocol affirms that "the recruitment, transportation, transfer, harbouring or receipt of a child for the purpose of exploitation shall be considered trafficking in persons even if this does not involve any of the means set forth in sub-paragraph (a) of this article." With this definition the transportation of a child to an urban centre for the purposes of begging constitutes trafficking regardless of whether this process was enforced by a third party or family member. The severity of this form of trafficking is starting to gain global recognition, with the International Organization for Migration, the European Union, the ILO, and the United Nations, among others, beginning to emphasise its pertinence.

Studies have shown that children forced into begging primarily receive little to no education, with upwards of sixteen hours a day dedicated to time on the streets. With education being a leading method in escaping poverty child beggars have been shown to engage in a cyclical process of continuing this practice cross-generationally. Interviews conducted by UNICEF (2000) show that children who beg have little hope for the future and do not believe their circumstances will improve. Children who work on the streets typically have little or no knowledge of their rights, leaving them especially susceptible to exploitation both as juveniles and later as adults. Children who beg have also been found by UNICEF (2000) to have much higher instances of HIV infection due to lack of awareness and supervision on the streets. According to the Protocol to Prevent, Suppress and Punish Trafficking in Persons, Especially Women and Children (2000), child trafficking is the recruitment, transportation, transfer, harbouring or receipt of children for the purpose of exploitation. It is a violation of their rights, their well-being and denies them the opportunity to reach their full potential.

The European Union's Brussels Declaration on Preventing and Combating Trafficking includes child begging as one form of trafficking, stating: "Trafficking in human beings is an abhorrent and worrying phenomenon involving coercive sexual exploitation, labour exploitation in conditions akin to slavery, exploitation in begging and juvenile delinquency as well as domestic servitude." This issue is especially difficult to regulate given that forced begging is often imposed by family members, with parental power leveraged over a child to ensure that begging is carried out.

Rachel Williams on Thursday 3rd July 2008 reported in *The Guardian* that:

> Teenage girls born in Britain are being trafficked for sexual exploitation within the UK, police said yesterday, adding that children are being groomed by men acting as boyfriends who carry out the abuse and then take the youngsters to other towns for further exploitation. Officers fear that as many as 33 girls between the ages of 12 and 15 could have been involved in a case uncovered in Sheffield last year. Only one, a 15-year-old, was willing to give evidence in court, but following that a 23-year-old man was jailed for 10 years for serious sexual offences which included rape of a child. Five other men faced deportation procedures. The victims were living in Local Authority care or with their families. Officers at the UK Human Trafficking Centre (UKHTC) said they had heard reports of girls as young as 12 being forced to perform sexual acts up to 20 times a night. The Home Office Minister Vernon Coaker said it was difficult to establish the scale of internal trafficking. It is something that increasingly people are raising and we are trying to get a better understanding of what exactly is taking place. People groom them, get their trust and then betray that trust. Police have adopted terms like "lover boy" to describe the way older men at first act like an indulgent boyfriend, showering the young girls with drugs and gifts including money and jewellery.

According to the UKHTC, the girls are encouraged to go missing from home and to spend more and more time with their boyfriends, who eventually start controlling them with threats and violence. At this stage the children will be taken to other locations in the UK, introduced to other groups of men and asked by the boyfriend to give the others sexual favours, because they are his friend. Terrified and under the control of the boyfriend, the girl feels unable to refuse. Some girls have described being subjected to extreme violence, including rape, while others have reported that they were used to transport and deal drugs.

The details on internal trafficking emerged as the government revealed the biggest crackdown yet on traffickers bringing people into the UK to work in the sex industry. In July 2008 Tim Brain, the chief constable of Gloucester, reported that there were now 18,000 victims of trafficking in the UK and that this included under-age girls. *The Guardian* in September 2008 reported that estimates by police suggest there could be as many 18,000 trafficking victims being forced to work as prostitutes in the UK. About 167 victims, including thirteen children aged between fourteen and seventeen, were rescued across Britain and Ireland, and 528 suspected traffickers were arrested during the six months of Operation Pentameter 2, which ended earlier that year. The majority of the victims came from China and south-east Asia, with a smaller number from Eastern Europe. Three children were found who had been trafficked for forced labour. More than £500,000 in cash has been recovered from those arrested, and court orders are in place to keep further criminal assets worth more than £3,000,000. More than eighty people were charged with various offences and there have been twenty-four convictions, although only two people have been found guilty of human trafficking. Measures have been taken to tackle the problem of trafficked children being forced into criminal activities, including working in cannabis farms, and being brought to Britain to make fraudulent welfare claims have been added to the government's action plan.

Children of trafficking are also to be granted a forty-five day period of grace after their rescue, even if they are in the country illegally. In many cases the children will get a one-year temporary residency permit. The Home Office had already pledged to ratify a European agreement to give a period of thirty days' grace. Coaker also admitted that the authorities were struggling to combat the problem of children disappearing after being rescued from the hands of suspected traffickers. On 23rd Apr 2008 *The Guardian* revealed this year that more than 400 foreign children, many suspected of being trafficked into the sex or drug trade, had gone missing from Local Authority care.

Some youngsters go to extraordinary lengths to get away from the people trying to protect them, having been deceived into believing they were accompanied into the country in their best interests. Coaker said: "This is a huge issue, to support them and keep them safe" he said, "Short of locking them up in protective custody, we're struggling. We're looking to see what we can do to keep children safer."

Gloucestershire's chief constable, Tim Brain, who coordinated Pentameter 2, said the investigation had revealed a large number of brothels in ordinary suburban flats and houses. Of more than 800 premises visited, nearly 600 were residential, while 157 were massage parlours, saunas, and nail bars. "It is likely that in future police investigations will have to consider all kinds of premises", Brain said. The residential locations were "very, very ordinary". He added: "In some of the cases the neighbours who live nearby have not actually suspected any kind of unusual activity." The first phase of Pentameter, in 2006, rescued eighty-eight victims and made 232 arrests. Brain said: "The increase in arrests is good news in terms of police and partner agency effectiveness, but it does mean that we still have an insidious problem in the heart of our society." Coaker said there was no evidence to suggest trafficking to Britain was increasing. Although the number of arrests and victims found in the latest operation had risen, the period of the operation was twice as long.

While recent research has yielded information on the nature of child trafficking, still little is known about its magnitude. The ILO's in 2002 estimation of 1.2 million children being trafficked each year remains the reference (Every Child Counts, New Global estimate on Child Labour). UNICEF works with development partners, governments, and non-governmental organisations on all aspects of anti-trafficking responses—prevention, protection, and prosecution—and supports evidence-based research to strengthen interventions.

To reduce vulnerabilities that make children susceptible to trafficking, UNICEF assists governments in strengthening laws, policies, and services including legislative reviews and reforms, establishing minimum labour standards, and supporting access to education. UNICEF also works with communities to change norms and practices that exacerbate children's vulnerabilities to trafficking. Protecting trafficked children requires timely victim identification, placing them in a safe environment, providing them with social services, health care, psychosocial support, and reintegration with family and community, if it is proven to be in their best interest. UNICEF assists by supporting training of professionals working with children including social workers, health workers, police and border officials to effectively deal with trafficking. Additionally, UNICEF supports governments in setting standards in dealing with child trafficking such as developing and training responsible personnel on child friendly interviewing techniques.

Just as great diversity exists amongst refugee experiences, so, too, does such range exist for child refugees, whether arriving with family or unaccompanied. Some children we work with have endured sexual exploitation and trafficking or were trafficked to the UK as a child on a visa to live with relatives in private fostering arrangements. It is difficult to estimate the exact number of non-British children in the UK in private fostering placements. Although many private fostering arrangements will provide children with the care they need, we have worked with many children in private fostering arrangements who have been harmed, exploited through domestic servitude or labour or abused for benefit fraud by extended family members and sexual exploitation (Wirtz, 2009).

So, the challenges for refugee young people can be enormous; their experience of persecution, torture, and flight from their native countries can cause intense trauma and a sense of loss—the loss of identity and sometimes the loss of self, and having constant fear, fear of rejection and further abuse. However, additional challenges also arise in their host country which consequently disrupts the wellbeing and settlement process for these vulnerable individuals.

CHAPTER TEN

Community engagement

What is community engagement and what does good engagement look like? In reference to refugee children and young people the first thing surely would be communities' active participation as a whole, including local residents and community groups. It is necessary to develop a range of interactions which are suitable, indeed useful for all parties involved, such as simple information sharing through supporting community activities, and creating connections with existing organisations at the intersection of the local, national and international services for the exchange and dissemination of knowledge. Community engagement strategies may be deployed to hand some of the responsibility from the State to local communities and non-statutory organisations involving the dissemination and publication of good practice and useful projects in developing countries. We need to rethink how we talk about refugee children's needs who have been tortured and to engage with our local and global communities for the rehabilitation and care of those children. This book addresses issues that are provocative, critical, and challenging, and which need careful examination to learn best practices, taking into consideration community engagement as one of the major points. Focusing on the front lines in communities and the extraordinary diversity within each community is needed to uncover best strategies that seek to provide appropriate support to children who have been tortured and seek sanctuary. Based on these strategies, the structure of services needs to take into consideration the characteristics of each individual child and the community the child is from, indeed the common culture and traditions, knowledge and the decisions that affect the child's life.

Having said this, there is the real fact of spending and the way central and local governments make decisions to commission services in the community. Improved literacy among refugee children and families by provision of mentoring as extra curriculum complimentary support helps to improve their English language skills as well as support children in their process of integration, adaptation of new cultural environments and acculturation. One of the issues that should be taken into account in the consideration of cost-effectiveness of services is the outcome. This is more than simply the monetary amount expended. Other factors should be considered in terms of providing lasting, sustainable, and positive outcomes. Such an approach can benefit a wide range of social, health and education service costs such as:

- Fewer admissions to A&E with psychosomatic symptoms brought on by the anxiety due to the past trauma of children and young people;
- Fewer visits to GP surgeries presenting psychosomatic symptoms;
- Preventing psychotic breakdowns among young refugees and asylum seekers, alleviating the burden on psychiatric services;
- Fewer family or foster care breakdowns through liaison with Social Services, and mental health services. This will benefit other services such as hospitals, schools, police, child protection, and court proceedings;
- Less crime, through the provision of a safe space where children and young people can deal with their anxiety and emotional distress.

However, it is important to note that the frequent changes to asylum legislation and policy can make it difficult for children and young people and their families to settle in their new environment. The changing variables that impact the lives of refugees and asylum seeker children and young people as they try to resettle are important to take into account for the provision of services.

An outcome: Refugee Therapy Centre

A young woman I worked with for some time in her adolescence stood up at an event and told people in attendance that:

> We should not forget that most people like me and some of you here today were born and grew up in countries in which women, girls, men, and boys are not treated equally and without discrimination, and many woman like my mother and I have to escape persecution, torture, and discrimination. Therefore I think efforts of the wonderful people who helped me must continue in order to help refugee women and girls to deal with the memory of torture and trauma and to make progress in the new environment. Having had help myself—thanks to my doctor I learned to understand that I could not jump and I need to keep calm and take one step at a time to deal with the memory that was hunting me. I have received help and support from my doctor in 2007. I was only fourteen years old, a sad, confused, and angry unaccompanied minor living with my foster carer who I thought at the time did not care about me. I had a lovely social worker when I first arrived in the UK who I built a very nice and safe relationship, but after a few months I didn't see her anymore and was visited by another social worker without any goodbye or prior notice.
>
> I was trafficked to the UK by a woman who took a lot of money and promised my family a good life, education, and bright future for me in the UK. When I first arrived I was used as a domestic servant at this lady's house. Later her brother started abusing me and after a very short period used me sexually, forcing me to sleep with many other men he said were his friends. The first time I told him that I did not want to do it and if he forced me I would tell the social worker or someone, and he beat me so badly that I thought I would die. After that I was locked in a house for months. One day I escaped. I was on the street for ages. I don't know exactly how long. I was very scared but did not want to go back to that house anymore. One day while I was walking in Finsbury Park I was caught by two community police officers. I told them my problem and they took me to the police station, and there I met my social worker and then I was in foster care that night. I felt safe and looked after for the first time. I had a shower and slept in bed. That night

I had time to think that I was new to the country, had no family or friends and spoke very little English. I felt sad, and cried myself to sleep, but I was not scared of a big man coming to the kitchen and raping me as had happened before in that family's house.

My social worker talked to me about referring me to get help with my fear, anxiety, and nightmares. I first met my doctor, who is sitting here today but told me not to mention her name, and that week she provided me with a lovely mentor Parisa, a very nice young lady who was a medical student who was seeing me every Wednesday to help me with my English, and also help me to understand my other school work. I really loved her and will love her for the rest of my life. I trusted her with everything. I also was seeing my doctor on the same day just before my mentoring session. So, you can imagine, Wednesday was the highlight of my week and I could not wait to finish school and rush to my sessions. Before I knew it, I was speaking perfect English. My school teachers were surprised that I developed my academic work so fast. I also started talking with my peers and teachers and developed good friendships with some of my classmates. My mentor and also my doctor both helped me to learn how to make friends at school and with other foster children and to feel connected. Some of the friends I have continued to stay in touch with today and two of my best friends are amongst them. I gradually built my confidence and achieved a good result in my education. I am grateful not only to my doctor who helped me to be the person I am today, but I am sure she has helped many other children like me. I think if I can do one per cent of what she has done for me for other young children I will be pleased with myself and I have learned to love and to feel loved, to have hope, compassion and humility. I learned not to be selfish and I learned so much about myself and others.

I am now studying medicine and this I owe to my doctor who gave me confidence and encouraged me to trust my ability. When I was on my third year I applied to become a volunteer mentor and I am so pleased to have been given an opportunity to mentor other young refugees, giving back something small. Initially when I applied to join the Centre as a volunteer mentor my doctor met with me and suggested that I should consider doing volunteer work in another similar organisation but left the decision to me. I decided to stay and I am thankful to her once again for being respectful of

what I wanted rather than being rejected. Every week when I come
to the Centre and see her door is closed, my immediate feeling is
sadness, like a little girl who misses her mum, but when I think
what she has done and is doing I feel her presence and her legacy
that I know I am a part of, as she taught me to recognise and focus
on the ability of my mind and matter and comfort of my heart—so
my momentary sadness of missing her immediately turns to the
feeling of being contained, self-assured, useful, and happy.

This young woman came to the UK as unaccompanied minor.

Children's resilience in adverse situations

There is a body of research that questions western orthodox medical
and therapeutic models of intervention in helping children of refugees who have endured torture, adversity, separation, and forms of
human right violations and whose worlds have been unsafe, unpredict-
able, confusing, and full of fear and uncertainty. The conditions these
children are in are intrinsically unjustifiable, unstable, and frightening,
exemplifying uncertainty and ambiguity. For many children there is no
possibility, no regularity, no consistency, no stability and no strength.
So, by nature of such conditions, these children's experiences will be far
from the normal developmental process, causing the developments of
strength of mind and will to be disrupted. In order for children to flour-
ish, they need enduring security and stability in their social environment, which many children have lost by the very fact that they are here
as refugees. The question remains, however, whether the UK, or indeed
other countries that children of refugees end up in, can provide a containing and caring environment for these children to enable them to
pick up from where they left off by the forced conditions of their lives.

Despite the remaining gaps in the UK's ability to provide such environments, this is not to suggest that there are no appropriate and useful
services available that identify the gaps and in a small way intend to
fill them. My question however, is whether children services, such as
CAMHS in the UK, have sufficient resources to provide intercultural
interventions and facilitate environmental forces that are positive and
healthy for children of refugees. Young children are reliant on the
resourcefulness of adults for their care and safety. If there is no responsible loving and caring adult available as children get older, they may

lack the competence, the empathic capacity, creativity and resiliency to deal with difficult situations, especially if they have been exposed to multiple stressors which have prevented the development of psychic space and sense of self.

Having said this, I do not intend to generalise that childhood and adolescent development is universal without cultural factors. Some cultures do provide a community environment that without too much effort creates psychological resourcefulness for children of all age groups and the social competencies of those beyond early childhood to adult life. Cultural values bring together and build a persistent set of rules accepted by a particular society, and can provide insights into how children perceive and process discontinuities, inconsistencies, and conflicts in their environment. Valuing stability in the development and wellbeing of children has given way to a far more dynamic view, emphasising the active, constructive nature of human development and the dynamic nature of relating to self and others.

For children of refugees to engage with their new environment they must interpret the new world around them, be educated and encouraged to make choices, given opportunities to define their identities, be supported to manage crises, and reach decisions, and informed and inspired to relate to others. The dynamic nature of child development and children's resiliency to cope with trauma and adversity of torture and other forms of violations, challenges the possible tokenistic assumption that children of refugees are helpless and vulnerable. Many children of refugees have considerable inner resources for coping with the memory of trauma they have endured in their life, but effects of torture are not easy to cope with without timely support. Fears of permanent psychological difficulty therefore can get in the way of positive development and creates vulnerability for negative changes and choice of life styles. Such uncertainty and confusion can lead to psychological restraint and lock down for many children which could carry into adulthood. Another issue that we need to be mindful about is the possibility that consciously or unconsciously through our interactions with children of refugees, we may project our vulnerabilities to be theirs or imagine that they must be far more vulnerable than they truly are, ultimately planning our intervention based on our assumptions and around our own needs, rather than theirs. While emphasising the needs of children of refugees who have experienced multiple stressors that are likely to have a cumulative psychological effect which may ultimately overwhelm their coping capacity, we also must take into consideration that, in general, well-adjusted, well-cared for children rarely lose their resiliency when they endure trauma. Of course the validity of children of refugees' experiences should be an integral part of interventions. An appropriate intercultural intervention should not be based on a clinician's fixed opinions about children, or policies and involvements that treat children as the objects of inappropriate adult decisions. Rather, interventions should be focused around children as social subjects with valid insights and perspectives of their own. So, an assessment of children of refugees should not totally rely on adults' views, and children's own perspectives should be encouraged, explored and taken with respect. This is not to indicate that a source of help in dealing with a problem from a legally responsible adult's knowledge and insight of children's experiences should be dismissed; but that we need to take into consideration the fact that an adult may be affected more greatly or less than the child within the same traumatic encounter. Sometimes the concern is that children may not tell the truth about their age, specifically adolescents. Although it is important to look at the matter, it is imperative to ensure that children are not harmed by intrusive interviews or measures intended to assist the interview (i.e., dental examination). The age assessment is a complex issue that has significant and often detrimental consequences for the children and young people of refugees. It is particularly concerning that in practice many age assessments are not properly planned, improvised and may be based on rushed judgements that are undertaken by those with no or limited or lack of knowledge and insight about biological and sociocultural factors of children (I worked with a fourteen year old Afghan boy who was so angry for not being believed and felt humiliated and abused by the process of age assessment. Of course the professional who raised the concern observed this young boy shaving his dark facial hair, which is quite unusual in a white western boy of a similar age). The assessments of age are requested and carried out with great focus on attempts to determine a child's exact age and this needs to be communicated with the child in a calm and educational manner so the child does not feel unbelieved or that he is being accused of lying, even though age assessment is not universally accurate or rigorous science.

Undoubtedly, children cannot always express themselves in a manner that appears consistent and logical, but then neither do some adults who have been tortured. Even so, a refined adaptation of culturally and linguistically appropriate services will support the person to communicate better. Furthermore, an age appropriate interview can help a child or a young person to call forth what has happened to her or him and conjure up the memory of torture as he or she can remembers. This could create a positivist paradigm which relies less on the preconceptions of the examiner and more on the perspectives or actual experiences of the child being interviewed. However, children's concepts, perceptions and understandings are likely to be more relevant or at least significant to the situation. I am not suggesting that children of refugees are exceptional or out of the ordinary creatures inhabiting their own universe, immune to the kinds of grief and suffering of others, but intend to highlight that their anxieties may differ from those working with them or caring for them. Indeed, professionals may be totally unaware about what is really troubling the child. So, being patient and listening to children is the most effective way to brings satisfactory results.

There is a great need for research that takes into consideration children's perspectives in order to better envisage the impact of exposure to torture and other forms of trauma and adversity. For example, among those children who do suffer serious or prolonged psychological and emotional distress, a significant proportion have not experienced a major hardship or catastrophe, but less dramatic circumstances that are more deleterious and unfulfilling than tragic, catastrophic persecutions and torture. Sometimes the most devastating situations are those involving stealthy but dangerous torture, hardships, and deprivations, such as constant humiliation, social isolation, or poverty related to long term nutrition and food depravations in captivity. In terms of the physical impact, far more children capitulate to secondary effects of starvation than torture. Such experience may lead to humiliation and guilt, and consequently loss of the secure sense of self, can be leading to a highly stressful adulthoods as well as childhood disruptions. These children's experiences should not be disregarded, as it risks pursuing misplaced activities. Children's real problems, concerns, and confusions should be given space for expression for gaining insight into their feelings and to make sense of their experiences. This suggests that we as professionals need to temper our assumption of childhood irrationality and adult expertise with some humanity and humility; as well as to recognise the need for new methods for intercultural ways of working and adopt methodologies that are child-centred, and are sensitive to cultural context, looking specifically at the traumatic experiences of children of refugees.

Common presenting problems in children of refugees and young people include:

- Anxiety and depression;
- Anger that may be presented as "aggressive and violent behaviour"— acting out;
- Withdrawal;
- Impaired social/psychological development & educational achievement;
- Difficulties in relating to other and making friends;
- Physical complaints e.g., chronic pain, headaches;
- Sleeping problems (sleeplessness, flashbacks, nightmares);
- Difficulty settling and adjusting into new environment;
- Feelings of helplessness and hopelessness;
- Problems with concentration and memory;
- Recurrent feelings of mistrust;
- Hyperactivity;
- Juvenile Delinquency;
- Suicide and deliberate self-harm;
- Disorganised attachment;
- Identity problems;
- Eating problems—anorexia nervosa, bulimia.

If these difficulties are left unattended, they can lead to serious mental health problems in later life. But, if children of refugees and their families are helped early enough, much needless emotional suffering and intellectual underperformance can be prevented. It is important to remember that the problems that children of refugees may present should not be seen as totally different and separate from those of other children who may be unhappy and distressed. Also, it is important to note that children of refugees come from a wide range of cultures and have had very varied experiences; therefore they present their needs and difficulties in a variety of ways. There is no one recognisable pattern of behaviour. However, it is useful to think about some of the difficult past experiences which some children continue to be affected by. Simply understanding a child's distress is very important. Children who have been hurt and have lost so much are not going to start feeling good very quickly. We may not be able to make them feel better straight away, but we can help them to cope with their feelings and provide help with respect, at the child's own pace.

One of the major obstacles and anxiety creating matters is restrictive asylum policies. These are a preventing factor in a young person's ability to negotiate new challenges in their new circumstances and possibly for some, a totally new environment. There is a need for empirical research, specifically focusing on relationships between trauma in the past and post-migratory traumas in general, and specifically the gap in services for children reaching adult age. The high levels of exposure to traumatic events prior to coming to the host country—then a sudden asylum-seeking process combined with vulnerability are the strongest predictors of psychological problems in young refugees. My focus here has therefore been to look at the meaning of trauma, the legal dimensions of the life of refugee children and to expand a possible classification of traumatic events that have an impact on an individual child's and young person's functioning in general, with specific reference to children of refugees and asylum seekers from human right perspectives. I start with a description of trauma to offer a general understanding of the term, looking at possible causes, various kinds, its dynamics, its mechanisms, and the diverse areas of functioning that trauma potentially impacts on, specifically children of refugees' experiences of trauma, not just in the country of origin or challenges during the escape to safety, but the further stresses in the process of immigration and life in the new environment. I look at the consequences of trauma and the relevance of these in resilience, with a brief discussion about post-traumatic stress disorder (PTSD). However, post-trauma, or better to say, on-going traumatic stresses in the lives of children of refugees are different from the ordinary psychiatric formulation. Most outcomes of vulnerability in children of refugees by and large represent intra-psychic and the world dissolution that is influenced by external challenging or oppressive circumstances of which the asylum-seeking system is one of the major factors. Emphasis throughout is given to the fact that people in general and children and young people specifically have subjective reactions to objective events—meaning that no two children or young people will experience or respond to a stressor of environmental trauma in the same way—but they are affected one way or another.

Despite growing recognition of the negative impact of ever rigorous and stern asylum-seeking processes employed by the UK and other western governments, when children reach adult age and psychological conceptualisations of distress, these issues continue to create obstacles by enforcing the dominating immigration matters that create further post-migratory stress and traumatisation for young people who have just reached an adult age. Children are considered adults by law just over night and officially become asylum seekers, enduring a range of post-migratory traumas relating to resettlement challenges, yet even more social isolation and broken attachments (with foster carers or social workers), economic deprivation, and lack of understanding of the strange territory of immigrations and restrictive asylum legislation.

One example is the situation in Syria and what is happening to children in the conflict. The conflict started with anti-government peaceful demonstrations in March of 2011 as part of the Arab Spring activity, but very quickly this escalated into violent crackdown, both by government and rebels. By July 2011, army rebels had loosely organised the Free Syrian Army and many civilian Syrians took up arms to join the opposition. Divisions between secular and Islamist fighters, and between ethnic groups, continue to complicate the politics of the conflict. The full-blown civil war has killed over 220,000 people, half of whom are believed to be civilians; bombings are damaging cities and killing people in cities and horrific human rights violations have been prevalent. Basic necessities like food, water and medical care are insufficient and inadequate. The UN estimates that 6.6 million people are internally displaced. When you also consider refugees, more than half of the country's pre-war population of 23 million is in need of urgent humanitarian assistance, whether they still remain in the country or have escaped across the borders.

On 23rd August 2013, UNHCR reported that 1 million Syrian children had been forced to flee their homes as refugees and most had arrived in Lebanon, Jordan, Turkey, Iraq, and Egypt. The report indicated that half of all refugees fleeing the Syrian conflict were children under the age of 18, and of those 740,000 were under the age of eleven.

UNICEF Executive Director Anthony Lake said:

> One millionth child refugee is not just another number. This is a real child ripped from home, maybe even from a family, facing horrors we can only begin to comprehend. [...] We must all share the shame

because while we work to alleviate the suffering of those affected
by this crisis, the global community has failed in its responsibility to
this child. We should stop and ask ourselves how, in all conscience,
we can continue to fail the children of Syria.

António Guterres (2015), High Commissioner of the UN Refugee
Agency (UNHCR) said that, "What is at stake is nothing less than the
survival and wellbeing of a generation of innocents", he further indicates that, "The youth of Syria are losing their homes, their family members and their futures. Even after they have crossed a border to safety,
they are traumatised, depressed and in need of a reason for hope."

According to the Office of the High Commissioner for Human Rights,
up until 2013, some 7,000 children were killed during the conflict in
Syria. UNHCR and UNICEF in 2013 also estimated that more than two
million children had been internally displaced within Syria. The physical upheaval, fear, stress, and trauma experienced by so many children
accounts for just part of the human crisis. Both agencies also highlight
the threats to children of refugees from child labour, early marriage and
the potential for sexual exploitation and trafficking. It is reported that
more than 3,500 children in Jordan, Lebanon, and Iraq have crossed
Syria. The UNHCR ensures that refugee families and children live in
some form of safe shelter. More than 1.3 million children in refugee
and host communities in neighbouring countries have been vaccinated
against measles in 2015 with the support of UNICEF and its partners.
Nearly 167,000 children of refugees have received psychosocial assistance; more than 118,000 children have been able to maintain their education inside and out of formal schools.

The situation in Syria has created a prevalence of trauma for children
within the regions affected. Large numbers of children have witnessed
killings, torture, and other atrocities in the country's conflict, as well as
suffering the extreme poverty of refugee camps. No child should ever
see the horrors of torture, murder, and terror being inflicted on people.
The pilfering of childhood for the children exposed to war is a serious
crime against humanity, violating the human rights of that child. Children who have been exposed or experienced first-hand the horror of
war require specialist psychological support to come to terms with their
shocking experiences, as well as an opportunity to tell their narratives
and tell their stories, and to be heard, and receive appropriate documented support so that there may be the possibility for accountability

within national or international tribunals. World Vision, on their web-site, reported that with the Syria crisis 13.5 million people in Syria need humanitarian assistance, there are 4.3 million Syrians refugees, and 6.6 million are displaced within Syria; half are children. Most Syrian refugees remain in the Middle East: in Turkey, Lebanon, Jordan, Iraq, and Egypt, and only less than ten per cent of the refugees have travelled to Europe (Omer, 2015).

Syrians are fleeing due to violence they have been experiencing since the Syrian civil war began. The World Vision report suggests according to the Syrian Observatory for Human Rights that 320,000 people have been killed, including 12,000 children, and around 1.5 million people have been wounded or permanently disabled. Infrastructure within Syria including health care, education systems, and other services has been destroyed and the country's economy is shattered. Syrian children's hope for a better future is destroyed and many lost parents or their loved ones, suffered injuries, missed years of schooling, and witnessed killing and brutality. Children and young people during the conflicts are forcibly recruited to serve as fighters and human shields. Syrians fleeing conflict need assistance because they cannot sustain their lives without food, clothing, health assistance, and secure home. In some places they are deprived of supplies of clean water, as well as sanitation facilities. Children do not have a safe environment nor a chance to play or access education facilities, and due to the increased conflicts in Syria their parents are deprived of employment.

According to the World Vision reports, Turkey is hosting more than 1.9 million Syrian refugees. Iraq, despite many years of facing its own armed conflict, is hosting over 250,000 Syrians, Lebanon is hosting more than 1.1 million refugees; around 630,000 refugees have settled in Jordan, mostly with host families or in rented accommodations, 80,000 live in Za'atari, a camp near the northern border with Syria, and about 23,700 live in another camp, Azraq. Due to the high number and the lack of appropriate resources many have taken up residence in abandoned buildings, sheds, spare rooms, garages, and in tent settlements on vacant land.

In all these places every single person can be at risk, but children specifically are at risk to starvation or malnutrition and can become ill due to diseases brought on by lack of sanitation. Some children have to work in dangerous or demeaning circumstances for little pay to support their families. Those and some other children are vulnerable to physical, psychological, and sexual abuse and exploitation in unfamiliar and over-crowded conditions. Without adequate income to support their families and fearful of their daughters being molested, parents and especially single mothers may feel compelled to arrange marriage for their girls, in some cases as young as twelve or thirteen years old. The UN children's agency reported that the war reversed ten years of progress in education for Syrian children and between 2 to 3 million Syrian children are not attending school (Omer, 2015, in: *World Vision Magazine*).

Every year of the conflict has seen an exponential growth in refugees. In 2012, there were 100,000 refugees. By April 2013, there were 800,000. That doubled to 1.6 million in less than four months. There are now 4.3 million Syrians scattered throughout the region, making them the world's largest refugee population under the United Nations' mandate. In October 2015, when Russia decided and began launching airstrikes at ISIS targets in Syria, more Syrians were forced to flee for safety. This also makes delivery of humanitarian aid to Syrian civilians more challenging than it already was before. The UN predicts there could be 4.7 million registered Syrian refugees by the end of 2016, the worst situation for Syrian people and the larger migration and evacuation since the Rwandan genocide.

According to a UN report published at the end of 2015, more than 60 million people worldwide were forced to leave their homes only during 2015, with war and other violent conflicts being the main motivating factors. This number shows the highest ever published in history. It indicated that about one in every 122 of the world's population has now left their original habitual living place as a refugee. In recent years, Syria's civil war has been the largest and fastest single driver of mass movement, around 4.2 million Syrians fled abroad from Damascus and elsewhere in the country by mid-2015, and further 7.6 million had been internally displaced. Other countries where as the result of conflicts have been generating refugees and add to the crises includes Ukraine, Afghanistan, Somalia, Iraq, South Sudan, Burundi, the Central African Republic, and the Democratic Republic of Congo.

Beyond Syria's recent event, looking at other conflict areas the UN Secretary General's report on "Children and Armed Conflict in Sudan" has highlighted that in 2007 and 2008 internally displaced children in Darfur faced the highest risk of rape and sexual violence (UNSC, 2007). One third of the thirty-four reported incidents, which the UN verified, were perpetrated against internally displaced children or occurred within the vicinity of an IDP camp. Girls were reported to be particularly at risk. One account was of a fifteen-year-old girl who was raped in January 2008 while collecting firewood with a group of women on the outskirts of their camp in Western Darfur. Tragically, this example is one of many, representative of the chronic victimisation of children living within this context.

A report (*British Journal of Sociology*, 2011) raises concerns over the abduction and sexual violence toward children in Darfur which, to a great extent, remains unreported in a large part due to social stigma attached to these crimes for the victims. Although some cases are confirmed as the result of investigations by the UN, the extent of the problem goes far beyond this. Social stigma, although perhaps a primary reason for underreporting of sexual crimes against children, is not a stand-alone barrier; corrupt officials, absence of adequate legal protections and access to effective statutory procedures are among additional obstacles to more accurate reporting, and thus justice and appropriate care for those affected. The 2011 report in the *British Journal of Sociology*, "The displaced and dispossessed of Darfur: Explaining the sources of a continuing state-led genocide", examines 1,000 interviews with Black African participants who fled from twenty-two villages in Darfur to several refugee camps. The report observes how attacks by state security men or Janjaweed (armed militia from ethnic Sudanese Arab tribes) intentionally targeted food and water sources to extricate Black Africans in Darfur from February 2003 to August 2004. The report explores links amongst these targeted attacks and the ethnic motivations behind them, indicating that attacks on food and water supplies made it 129 per cent more likely to be evacuated than burning their houses or killing people. Many important issues were addressed in this report, including the following:

- Refugees faced a 50% chance of attack on a daily basis from one or more of the different perpetrator groups at the height of the attacks in January-February 2004.
- The frequency of hearing racial epithets during an attack was 70% higher when it was led by the Janjaweed alone compared to official police forces; it was 80% higher when the Janjaweed and the Sudanese Government attacked together.

- Holding constant both the gender and age of respondents, the risk for being displaced was about 18% higher for the refugees who heard racial epithets during the attack.
- Risk of displacement was nearly 110% higher during a joint attack compared to when the police or Janjaweed acted alone, and 85% higher when Janjaweed forces attacked alone compared to when the attack was only perpetrated by the Sudanese Government forces.
- Five years after arriving in the camps, the average age of refugees was 37, and the random sample was nearly 60% female due to the high death rate among men of fighting age.

This report concludes that, "a key challenge in developing the international criminal law and research on the use of elimination strategies is the issue of intent." However, as indicated in the above analysis, the authors state that "there is abundant evidence of intent in Darfur" (*British Journal of Sociology*, 2011).

About half the rapes were carried out in Darfur by Janjaweed militiamen allied with the Sudanese government, and half were assaults by Chadian villagers near the UN refugee camp, usually when the women left to search for firewood or herd livestock, according to the report by the United States based group Physicians for Human Rights. The group got in touch with eighty-eight women to gather a clearer picture of the situation through a survey through camp leaders and by word of mouth. Recording rape and interviewing an injured party of sexual violence is considered to be problematic in Darfur's Muslim culture, where women fear being stigmatised and put to shame in their community. Further complicating the effort, women displaced inside Darfur live mostly in government-controlled parts and fear punishment.

The issue is highly quarrelsome and confrontational as the Sudanese government denies any systematic rape or violence against women and girls. One example of this abuse of children is in an interview with a nineteen-year-old woman from the Masalit tribe who recounted that when she was aged thirteen, four Arab gunmen on horseback attacked her family's farm in a Darfur village, shot and killed her father and raped her. She said that, "When they shot my father, they saw I was a little girl. I did not have any energy or force against them", she continued saying that, "they used me. I started bleeding. It was so painful. [...] I was sick for seven days. I could not stand up."

Physicians for Human Rights called for the prosecution of rape as a war crime and urged the International Criminal Court to issue warrants against Sudanese suspects. They also required better protection for refugees in the Chad camps by Chadian police and international peacekeepers. The group said three doctors and a human rights researcher interviewed eighty-eight women in the refugee camp in Farchana, where more than 20,000 Darfuris were observed by Chadian soldiers about thirty-four miles from Sudan's boundary .

The UNHCR Briefing Notes, on the 25th September 2015, provides a summary of the UNHCR spokesperson Mr Adrian Edwards' address at the press briefing, at the Palais des Nations in Geneva. Both Mr Edwards and Amin Awad, Director of the UNHCR Bureau for Middle East and North Africa, and the Regional Refugee Coordinator for the Syria Region, indicated that while more than 4 million Syrian refugees are in Syria's neighbouring countries, recent months have seen an increase in the number of Syrians seeking refuge further afield. They estimated that there have been almost 429,000 asylum applications by Syrians in Europe since 2011. Based on ongoing monitoring and assessments, surveys, focus group discussions, and daily interactions with refugees in Jordan, Lebanon, Egypt, and Iraq, UNHCR has identified seven principal factors behind this. The information gathered mainly applies to Syrians living as refugees in the region, rather than people moving directly out of Syria (UNHCR briefing note, 8th September 2015).

With Syria's crisis now into its fifth year and no sign of a resolution in prospect, hope is decreasing and diminishing for people and many are becoming refugees. Feelings of uncertainty about the future are compounded by despairing conditions, increasing a sense of hopelessness, despondency and anguish.

One of the obstacles to reporting on children's experiences of torture and human rights violation is often the lack of research to expose those who try to conceal tortures and atrocities that children suffer. Acknowledgement is needed by all organisations respecting, valuing, and working towards the implementation of human rights that uncovering and exposure of torture and abuse should become a priority. Monitoring of violations of child rights should be encouraged and commissioned, carried out by the local, regional, and international humanitarian and rehabilitation organisations. As clinicians, we must affirm a commitment to protect the rights of children which require our attention to the absenteeism of vigorous and robust clinical research into violations

perpetrated against refugee and displaced children, including unaccompanied minors, children of asylum seekers with family and those
under the care of social care systems.

Psychological intervention can play an important role in meeting the
needs of refugees and asylum seekers, their children and families. It
will help to combat the social exclusion. Culturally and linguistically
appropriate psychological support can help to lower levels of stress
associated with all aspects of immigration and integration as well as the
memory of previous experiences endured before arrival. When we let
down any child by not providing appropriate care and discipline, and
to help the child to understand boundaries and develop a strong sense
of self, we are setting society up for increased distress that may result
in delinquency.

Some refugee and asylum seeker parents express the concern that
their children are losing the language and culture of their home country, and this is causing weakening and decline of the family unit as well
as a confusion of identity and rejection of personal history and loved
ones. Some parents complain that their children are growing up with
different moral values to their own and become alienated from older
familial generations and devalue the family connections. There is some
evidence that supports this fear as the younger generation of children
learn English and adapt to the new culture quickly, and this can create
fear and anger in the parents. On the other hand, as indicated before,
some parents or close relatives of refugee children who don't speak
English use their young children as interpreters and translators without
recognising that children's understanding and level of language capacity is not at an adult level. This of course can be traumatic to children
and young people pushed into this position. As discussed before, with
more under-fives than in the general population as well as children
over five and adolescents, refugees and asylum seekers may have a
greater need for earlier provision of service. This puts children in equal
position to the general or indigenous population. The lack of training
and courses on refugee issues, language, working with interpreters and
anti-discriminatory practice, prevents professionals from meeting the
children of refugees' healthcare and emotional needs and it prevents
these children and families from using the healthcare professionals
within the community during the early years. Some of the key compo-
nents in provision of service delivery should be focusing on building a
sense of community that is safe and supportive; creating connections to

mainstream culture; and promoting much needed resources for appropriate intercultural treatment.

Violence against women and children is far too common and, in many parts of the world, still socially acceptable. Children and young people do not have the opportunity to escape abuse, because shelters and welfare resources are not available. Even where they may be available, these routes can often further victimise those they are ostensibly designed to protect and provide refuge for. Women often find themselves under considerable social pressure to keep families together regardless of the traumatic circumstances they themselves and their children are suffering as a result.

Apart from unaccompanied young people, there are other children of refugees with similar experiences of torture and human rights violations, which may also include experience of domestic violence and family break-down. Many refugee families and other immigrant children and families who came to the UK on a visa from Commonwealth countries like Jamaica, India or Pakistan and have overstayed, or those who were born in the UK to parents who came here on a visa but overstayed and have irregular immigration status, can prompt a variety of uncertainties and extreme challenges. Many in need of support are lone mothers with children who experience domestic violence or family breakdown. Data shows that mothers are often reluctant to leave abusive relationships because, having no recourse to public funds they are dependent on their partners financially, and often their immigration claim is in their partner's name. It is through pulling back the lens in this way that we are able to identify the nuances and shortcomings of the immigration system that often render children victims of on-going cycles of uncertainty and abuse.

CONCLUSION

Torture is a detestable crime under any circumstances. But the need for action is particularly critical when it is committed against children. And the unambiguous reality is that though people may not be aware of the extent of this crime as they do not often hear much about it, each day an immeasurable amount of children are subjected to torture or affected by witnessing the torture of their loved one and members of their community. The absolute prohibition of torture is specifically stated in the UN Convention on the Rights of the Child. But whilst the question of violence against children is more and more considered, discussed and concentrated on globally, in general there is trivial focus on and awareness about the particular needs and rights of children with respect to protection from torture and access to psychological support, rehabilitation and redress. This is particularly alarming, given that torture tends to have more harsh and long-lasting effects on children, often leading to the disruption and disturbance of the process of healthy psychological, emotional, and social development.

The UN Convention on the Rights of the Child (UNCRC) is particularly relevant to what is discussed in this book. Separated children are some of the most vulnerable people in society. The Article 22 of the UN Convention on the Rights of the Child indicates that:

> States Parties shall take appropriate measures to ensure that a child who is seeking refugee status or who is considered a refugee in accordance with applicable international or domestic law and procedures shall, whether unaccompanied or accompanied by his or her parents or by any other person, receive appropriate protection and humanitarian assistance in the enjoyment of applicable rights set forth in the present Convention and in other international human rights or humanitarian instruments to which the said States are Parties.
>
> For this purpose, States Parties shall provide, as they consider appropriate, co-operation in any efforts by the United Nations and other competent intergovernmental organizations or non-governmental organizations co-operating with the United Nations to protect and assist such a child and to trace the parents or other members of the family of any refugee child in order to obtain information necessary for reunification with his or her family. In cases where no parents or other members of the family can be found, the child shall be accorded the same protection as any other child permanently or temporarily deprived of his or her family environment for any reason, as set forth in the present Convention.

It is known that asylum seeking and refugee children and their families often have multiple and complex social needs. They may suffer from poverty, benefit restrictions, and a poor quality of temporary accommodation, all of which have a major impact on children and their carers. In the provision of services, an overview of the asylum and support systems for children should examine the interaction between these two. By focusing on procedures required of refugee young people during the process of immigration children should be given opportunity to be able to explore how best to respond to the difficulties they may be facing.

The Convention on the Rights of the Child is the most widely and rapidly ratified human rights treaty in history. The prohibition of torture, cruel, inhuman or degrading treatment and punishment has generated rich jurisprudence in the different human rights supervisory bodies. Under international law torture is considered a crime; it is absolutely prohibited and cannot and should not be justified under any circumstances. The prohibition of torture has accomplished the status of customary international and national law, it is binding for every state, regardless of whether or not it has ratified international treaties on the topic, so, the systematic and prevalent practice of torture constitutes a crime against humanity. Human rights instruments encompass provisions setting out the absolute prohibition of torture and provide protection for those detained by the state, obliging authorities to guarantee safeguards to individuals in their power. States should ensure minimum conditions in detention, in relation to, for instance, medical care. In addition, governments should provide safeguards during interrogation and detention and keep procedures for incarceration and interrogation under regular review.

Although the prohibition of torture is internationally accepted, torture and ill-treatment by those in power is still widely practiced. States are under an obligation to investigate allegations of torture and should promote the development and implementation of national and international standards which provide effective and enforceable remedies for people who have endured torture. States, individually and within the international community as a whole, must increase and intensify their efforts to eradicate torture world-wide and make the perpetrators and all those who aid and abet acts of torture liable for their actions.

The United Nations Convention Against Torture and Other Cruel, Inhuman or Degrading Treatment or Punishment (UNCAT) provides an exact definition of torture under international law and describes torture as:

> Any act by which severe pain or suffering, whether physical or mental, is intentionally inflicted on a person for such purposes as obtaining from him or a third person information or a confession, punishing him for an act he or a third person has committed or is suspected of having committed, or intimidating or coercing him or a third person, or for any reason based on discrimination of any kind, when such pain or suffering is inflicted by or at the instigation of or with the consent or acquiescence of a public official or other person acting in an official capacity. It does not include pain or suffering arising only from, inherent in or incidental to lawful sanctions.

Thus, the Convention Against Torture identifies three elements that, if combined, constitute torture:

1. Intentional infliction of severe pain or suffering;
2. For a specific purpose, such as to obtain information, as punishment or to intimidate, or for any reason based on discrimination;
3. By or at the instigation of or with the consent or acquiescence of State authorities.

The International Rehabilitation Council for Torture Victims is an important global organisation fighting torture and its members provide rehabilitation in more than 140 centres. They have indicated that some of the most common methods of physical torture include beating, electric shocks, stretching, submersion, suffocation, burns, rape, and sexual assault. Psychological forms of torture and ill-treatment, which very often have the most long-lasting consequences for people, include isolation, threats, humiliation, mock executions, mock amputations, and witnessing the torture of others.

The international community should place the torture of children onto the international human rights agenda, and ensure that this deep rooted problem of children who are subjected to torture in many countries all over the world is steadily combatted. Children who are being subjected to torture and ill treatment at the hands of their own governments and armed opposition groups need protection.

Drawing on evidence from the UN, inter-governmental bodies as well as a wide range of non-governmental organisations, this book identifies factors that increase the child's vulnerability to torture and ill-treatment including poverty, discrimination, conflict, family associations, and political alignments.

All states should ratify, implement, and enforce:

• The Convention against Torture and Other Cruel, Inhuman or Degrading Treatment or Punishment, including recognition of the right of states and individuals to petition the Committee against Torture;
• Regional human rights treaties, including the right of individual petition;
• The International Covenant for Civil and Political Rights, including the Optional Protocol which allows individual communications to be forwarded to the Human Rights Committee;

- The Convention on the Rights of the Child and the Optional Protocol on the Involvement of Children in Armed Conflict;
- The Rome Statute of the International Criminal Court.

States further should ensure that:

- Domestic legislation is brought into line with the Convention on the Rights of the Child and the Convention against Torture and takes urgent measures to ensure they become operational and well-known throughout society;
- Recognise each person below the age of eighteen years to be a child within the international definition;
- Establish alternatives to detention;
- Ensure that all children are registered upon birth;
- Abolish corporal punishment in all settings, in recognition of the fact that corporal punishment is not consistent with the Convention on the Rights of the Child and generally not accepted by international law.

As discussed throughout the book, there are very few statistics and there is no systematic documentation that exists on the subject that can address the issue globally. To address this gap, to highlight and bring the fact that children are tortured to global attention, and to enhance the support and rehabilitation of children who have endured torture, we need to make the campaign for eradicating torture of children one of the main focuses of our work globally. We need to ensure that appropriate services are able to reach children who have endured tortured either directly or by bearing witness. We need to provide space to help young people to regain their right to joy and dignity in life, develop capacity and to become resilient, positive and contributing members of society. While doing that, we also need to steer and lead preventative action to protect vulnerable children from torture. For this reason, we need standardised analysis involving a group of experts in the field to provide empirical data by leading and undertaking research for gathering evidence, developing knowledge, for sharing and dissemination of best practices.

To conclude, I would like to share a case of a young client I shall call Ahmed, that I have worked with. This is to illustrate that providing space for a child or young person to explore vulnerabilities resulting from torture and human rights violations can so easily lead the person to develop resilience and become a positive and contributing member of society. This kind of space can be effective only if professionals who are involved in health, education and law work together with the best interest of the child as their primary concern.

When he was thirteen years old Ahmed attempted suicide. He was found under the kitchen table by his older brother, and taken to the hospital immediately. While admitted he refused to talk to the professionals who were trying to help him, both clinicians and social workers. Ahmed's parents were killed in a war in his home country when he was eight years old, and his brother, six years older, became his carer before they eventually came to Britain, escaping from persecution. A child psychiatrist decided that he should be referred to the RTC. We talked over the phone about Ahmed's possible referral and agreed that the psychiatrist should be on call, if needed, and based on this arrangement, we accepted the referral.

In our first meeting with Ahmed and his brother it became apparent that he was often left alone and although he received material care, no one was involved in his life to provide for his level of emotional need. At that point Ahmed was not able to connect to his past or present; he seemed to be simply existing rather than living. His memories were distorted and perplexed and he had strong fears and a sense of hurting or losing his brother. His brother was very keen for both of them to focus on their education and advance their future prospects, with the hope that they could forget what had happened to them and not think about the painful memories of the past. Ahmed was cooperative and it was clear from our first encounter that he longed for adult female attention—a mother figure. In communication with his school's staff I came across quite a different view. They found him to be a difficult child, stubborn, and unresponsive to anyone and anything. They reported an incident when one of the boys in his year strangled him, and he did not move or retaliate, and when they wanted Ahmed to say what had happened, he did not respond. His teachers were concerned that some of his peers found him frightening because he would not engage with anyone. What struck me was his lack of response to bullying, his suicide attempt and its relation with his past experience.

In one of our meetings, he talked about the kindness of teachers here in London. He said he could not manage what was in his head, as he could "not finish thinking and would get confused and have bad feelings inside" him. He said that he "tried to listen and pay attention" but his "brain was confused and somewhere else" and he didn't understand what was happening. I realised that one of the reasons for his confusion was the fact that he did not have a vocabulary for his experiences and related concepts such as feeling different, afraid, terrified, anxious, sad, angry, disappointed, hurt or confused. It became more apparent that Ahmed needed a key adult who could set firm and clear boundaries with him to help him to feel contained, and with whom he could gradually built a trusting relationship. Ahmed's brother took the view that he simply had to get on with life. He, I thought, also needed help to change his manners towards Ahmed. To move away from this view seemed to raise too many difficult memories for Ahmed's brother. So I proposed that he also saw a therapist at the centre on a weekly basis to successfully engage with Ahmed and help him to recover. He agreed and I saw him every week, and in addition we met together with Ahmed once a month to discuss their progress. He admitted that he was keen on the idea and very grateful for the offer. He later told us that he did initially hesitate to ask for help for himself as he saw Ahmed as the priority and he did not want to be greedy and burden the system. He said this country had been very good to them and even though managing Ahmed was becoming more and more difficult for both of them, he thought he should cope on his own.

My work with Ahmed progressed rapidly and Ahmed became able to verbalise his feelings and thoughts. In one session he said:

> I used to think I would always have a happy life with my mum, dad, and my brother, but everything changed and my life became filled with torture and suffering. The difficulty started when my parents were killed. I didn't want to stay alive because, for me, life was over. I didn't want my life without my mother. I miss her and my dad. I am sorry to tell you all of this; I don't want you to think I am selfish. I feel bad about trying to kill myself because of how it affected my brother, but I cannot be happy with my life. My sad feeling is too strong for me to beat. I do not like to go to school or anywhere else. I do not like to go walking in the park on the weekend. I would be happier to stay at home because going to school is painful when everyone is talking about their parents. My brother told me that he wanted me to go to school and I have to go.

Three months into the therapy, Ahmed's deep depression and his social anxiety decreased and were steadily easing off. He settled quite well in school and was attending regularly without any problem. Apart from therapy I also offered him the chance to see a mentor on a weekly basis to help him understand his school work better. He was becoming more and more lively and was able to make friends at school. He was able to tell two of his close friends that he had lost his parents, but didn't tell them how. Through therapy, he gradually learned that he could say "I don't want to talk about it", if his fellow pupils were asking more. In the process Ahmed reached the stage when he actually looked forward to going to school. His feelings of guilt subsided and his attachment to his brother became healthier, rather than confused and ambivalent.

It is important to say that offering some recognition to Ahmed's complex feelings and providing some continuity in relationships with supportive adults provided him with the containing environment he needed to catch up to where he had left off during his development. Our monthly meetings with Ahmed and his brother helped the two brothers who cared for each other much learn that they could talk about what had happened to them without feeling guilty. Together in the group, we facilitated the possibility of talking about their experiences of torture and the loss of their parents and other loved ones. As a result, Ahmed began to settle down. Of course initially during the process, his progress was slow and we would occasionally go backwards. This was because as soon as the equilibrium was disturbed by even a minor change Ahmed would become withdrawn. But within a year we managed to work through it.

One year into therapy, Ahmed became a charming adolescent—a very tall and attractive fourteen year old young man. He developed the ability to show his appreciation for the help he had received, enabling him to heal from the memory of torture he had endured and the loss of his parents. In one of his last sessions he said:

> You know many people helped me and my brother after we lost our parents. With the advice of my psychiatrist I got a bit better. But the brightest hope for me has been the relationship I have with you and everyone here at the Refugee Therapy Centre, where my brother and I come every week. It is like a family home. I think I can come and visit all my life and you have to promise me you will never die on me—OK? Never-ever. [...] I want to thank you because you helped me like a good mother [...] my brother also feels good and happy and I have a brand new happy brother. When we are talking or playing together we think about you and the Centre. I want to thank everyone who helped me to become alive and enjoy my life. I thank our solicitor. I thank all people in this country for being so kind.

REFERENCES

Adelsberger, L. (2003). *Auschwitz—A Doctor's Story, 1895–1943 & 1945–1971*. International Bar Association: Northeastern University Press.

Akçam, T. (2013). *A Shameful Act: The Armenian Genocide and the Question of Turkish Responsibility*. New York: Metropolitan Books.

Alayarian, A. (2013). *Consequences of Denial: The Armenian Genocide*. London: Karnac.

Amnesty International (2003). United States of America, Unaccompanied Children in Immigration Detention. Amnesty International, p. 5.

Amnesty International (2007). Amnesty International Report 2007: The state of the world's human rights. Amnesty International.

Audiovisual Library of International Law, UN Convention against Torture, and other Cruel, Inhumane or Degrading Treatment or Punishment, Article 1, Paragraph 1.

BBC News (2002). Mozambique ex-rebel Renamo camp raided by Police.8th March 2012. Available at: http://www.bbc.co.uk/news/world-africa-17299319.

BBC News (2013). UK Border Agency "not good enough" and being scrapped. 26th March 2013. Available at: http://www.bbc.co.uk/news/uk-politics-21941395.

Booth, R. (2008). Lost 400 children may have been trafficked into sex or drugs trade. *The Guardian* 23rd Apr 2008. Available at: www.theguardian.com/society/2008/apr/23/childprotection.immigrationandpublicservices.

British Journal of Sociology (2011). The displaced and dispossessed of Darfur: Explaining the sources of a continuing state-led genocide. Available at: http://journalistsresource.org/studies/international/conflicts/darfur-sources-genocide.

Buffalo Human Rights Law Review, 14: 71–128; see also Kim, E. J. (2010). *Adopted territory: Transnational Korean adoptees and the politics of belonging. Durnham: Duke University Press Books.*

Cabinet Office (last updated 16th June 2009). Security in a global hub—Establishing the UK's new border arrangements. Available at: www.cabinetoffice.gov.uk/border_review.

Children Act Amendment (2004). C.31. Available at: www.legislation.gov.uk/ukpga/2004/31/contents. Accessed: 5th June 2013.

Cienfuegos, A. J., & Monelli C. (1983). The testimony of political repression as a therapeutic instrument. *Am J Orthopsychiatry, 53*(1): 43–51.

Demers, D. (2005), Terrorism, globalization and mass communication. In: *Handbook of Critical Public Relations*. Jacquie L'Etang, David McKie, Nancy Snow, & Jordi Xifra (Eds.). London: Routledge, pp. 193–214.

Dowdney, L. (2013). The Founder and Director of Fight for Peace. Available at: www.games4goodfoundation.com/.../beyond-sport-recognizes-luke-dowdney.

Equality and Human Rights Commission. Available at: www.equality-humanrights.com/sites/default/files/documents/humanrights/hrr_article_3.pdf, PP70. Accessed 29th November 2014.

European Convention on Human Rights (1950a). *Prohibition of torture, Article 3.* 4 November 1950. Available at: www.echr.coe.int/documents/convention_eng.pdf. Accessed on 14th January 2016.

European Convention on Human Rights (1950b). Right to respect for private and family life, Article 8. 4th November 1950. Available at: www.echr.coe.int/documents/convention_eng.pdf. Accessed on 14th January 2016.

European Social Charter (1961). Article 17: The right of mothers and children to social and economic protection, European Social Charter. http://conventions.coe.int/Treaty/en/Treaties/Html/035.htm.

Every Child Matters (2003). Presented to Parliament by the Chief Secretary to the Treasury by Command of Her Majesty September 2003.

Gentleman, A. (2012). Double death in asylum seeker family reveals gap in state benefits. *The Guardian 5th October 2012.* Available at: www.the-guardian.com/uk/2012/oct/05/immigration-children.

Government of Uganda; UNGASS Country Progress Report January 2008–December 2009. Submitted March 2010: http://data.unaids.org/pub/Report/2010/uganda_2010_country_progress_report_en.pdf.

Hate crime reduction strategy for London. Available at: www.london.gov.
uk/sites/default/.../mopac_hate_crime_reduction_strategy.

HM Government (2010). Working Together to Safeguard Children: a
guide to inter-agency working to safeguard and promote the welfare of
children, p. 34, 1.20. Available at: www.education.gov.uk/publications/
eOrderingDownload/00305-2010DOM-EN. Accessed on 11th April 2012.

Human Rights Review (2012). Equality and Human Rights Commission.
Available at: www.equalityhumanrights.com/en/publication.../human-
rights-review-2012.

International Rehabilitation Council for Torture Victims (IRCT). Accessed
23rd March 2012.

Johnson, J. G., Cohen, P., Brown, J., Smailes, E. M., & Bernstein, D. P. (1999).
Childhood maltreatment increases risk for personality disorders during
early adulthood. *Archives of General Psychiatry, 56*: 600–606.

Joseph, A. (2015). Revealed: Number of unaccompanied child migrants
being cared for by UK taxpayers has DOUBLED in the last three months
and six more arrive here alone EVERY day. *Mail Online* 28 August 2015.
Available at: http://www.dailymail.co.uk/news/article-3213973/Six-
unaccompanied-child-migrants-arrive-UK-day.html. Last accessed on
3rd October 2016.

Kingsley, C., & Mark, M. (2001). *Sacred Lives: Canadian Aboriginal Children
and Youth Speak Out About Sexual Exploitation.* Save the Children: Canada.

Laming, W. (2003). The Victoria Climbié Inquiry. In: The Government
Response to the Seventh Report from the Home Affairs Committee
Session (2013–2014 HC 71). The Stationery Office: London.

Littlewood, R., & Lipsedge, M. (1989). *Aliens and Alienists: Ethnic Minorities
and Psychiatry.* London: Unwin.

McCauley, C., & Mosalenko, S. (2009). *Friction: How Radicalization Happens
to Them and Us.* Oxford University Press, 2009. pp. 62–63.

Muñoz, E. L. (2002). The Unaccompanied Alien Child Protection Act. Available at: https://www.loc.gov/law/find/hearings/pdf/00104516609.pdf.

Nationality, Immigration and Asylum Act (2002); Section 55–57.

Omer, S. (2015). Syria Crisis and the Scars of War, conflict in Syria and neigh-
boring countries, a sense of childhood is slipping away. *World Vision
Magazine.* Available at: http://magazine.worldvision.org/stories/syria-
crisis-scars-of-war. Accessed on 6th January 2016.

Organization of African Unity (OAU), Convention Governing the Specific
Aspects of Refugee Problems in Africa ("OAU Convention"), 10th
September 1969, p. 1001 U.N.T.S. 45. Available at: http://www.refworld.
org/docid/3ae6b36018.html. Accessed 7th February 2014.

Parliamentary Ombudsman (2009–2010). Press release: Ombudsman pub-
lishes report on UK Border Agency. Available at: Ombudsman.org.uk.
Accessed on 12th April 2012.

Parliamentary Ombudsman (9th February 2010). Fast and Fair?—Report on UK Border Agency by the Parliamentary Ombudsman.

Refugee Council (2012). The facts about asylum. Refugee Council. Available at: www.refugeecouncil.org.uk/practice/basics/facts. Accessed 22nd November 2012.

Source: Stop sex with children website. Available at: www.stopsexwithkids.ca/app/en. Accessed on 14th September 2013.

Source: www.allafrica.com. Accessed 14th September 2013.

The Care Quality Commission (2009). Available at: www.cqc.org.uk/sites/default/files/media/documents/care_quality_commission_registration.pdf.

The Charter of the United Nations (1945). The Statute of the International Court of Justice. San Francisco. Available at: www.un.org/en/documents/charter/.

The Children Act (1989). Available at: http://www.legislation.gov.uk/ukpga/1989/41/contents.

The Children's Society (2007). Into the unknown, Children's journeys through the asylum process Report. Available at: www.childrenssociety.org.uk/sites/default/files/tcs/into-the-unknown--childrens-journeys-through-the-asylum-process--the-childrens-society.pdf.

The Constitution of Ireland (1937–1987). Article 129, Dublin: Institute of Public Administration: 1988.

The Crown Prosecution Service (2013). The code for crown prosecutors. January 2013. Available at: www.cps.gov.uk/publications/docs/code_2013_accessible_english.pdf. Accessed 21st January 2016.

The European Union's Brussels Declaration on Preventing and Combating Trafficking (29th Nov 2002). Available at: www.refworld.org/docid/4693ac222.html.

The Guardian (2008). Behavioural Science Operational Briefing Note: Understanding radicalization and violent extremism in the UK. Report BSU 02/2008. Available at: www.guardian.co.uk/uk/2008/aug/20/uksecurity.terrorism1. Accessed in August 2008.

The International Commission of Lawyers (2004) .The ICJ declaration on upholding human rights and the rule of law in combating terrorism, The Berlin Declaration, Berlin, Germany. *Human Rights Quarterly 27.1 (2005)*: 350–356.

The International Labour Organization (2002). *Every Child Counts: New Global estimate on Child Labour*. The International Labour Organization, Geneva. Available at: www.ilo.org/ipecinfo/product/viewProduct.do?productId=742.

The International Organization for Migration (1999). Worst Forms of Child Labour Convention. Available at: www.ilo.org/ipec/facts/ILOconventionsonchildlabour/lang—en/index.htm.

The Joint Committee on Human Rights. Twenty-sixth Report of Session 2005–2006. Available at: www.ohchr.org/EN/AboutUs/Pages/WhoWeAre.aspx.

UK Border Agency (26 March 2013). UK Parliament Hansard via They-WorkForYou.com. Retrieved 8th June 2013.

UK Border Agency Website (Former) (3 May 2013). "UK Border Agency's transition to Home Office". Retrieved 8 June 2013.

UK Home Office (2012). Asylum part 2: appeals, unaccompanied asylum-seeking children, age disputes and dependents, August 30th 2012. Available at: www.homeoffice.gov.uk/publications/science-research-statistics/research-statistics/immigration-asylum-research/immigration-q2-2012/asylum2-q2-2012. Accessed 5th November 2012.

UK Home Office (2013). The Home Office response to the Independent Chief Inspector's report. An inspection into the handling of asylum applications made by unaccompanied children. Available at: www.gov.uk/government/uploads/system/uploads/attachment_data/file/254526/Response_to_ICI_UASC_Report.pdf/. Accessed on 21st January 2016.

UK Home Office Statistics (GOV.UK). Available at: www.gov.uk/government/organisations/home-office/about/statistics.

UK Parliament (19th March 2013). The work of the UK Border Agency (July–September 2012)—Conclusions and recommendations.

UNHCR (2015). World at war. Available at: www.unhcr.org/statistics/country/556725e69/unhcr-global-trends-2014.html.

UNICEF (1989). United Nations Convention on the Rights of the Child. Available at: www.unicef.org.uk/Documents/Publication-pdfs/UNCRC_PRESS200910web.pdf.

UNICEF (2000). Guide for Monitoring and Evaluation. Organisation, monitoring and evaluation in UNICEF: the roles of UNICEF staff in country, regional and local. Available at: preval.org/documentos/00473.

UNICEF (2006). The State of the World's Children: Excluded and Invisible. UNICEF.

UNICEF (2014). Child labour and UNICEF in Action: Children at the Centre. Available at: www.unicef.org/protection/files/Child_Labour_and_UNICEF_in_Action.pdf.

United Nations (1984). Convention Against Torture and other Cruel, Inhumane or Degrading Treatment or Punishment. Equality and Human Rights Commission, Geneva.

United Nations (1990). Guidelines on the Role of Prosecutors. The Eighth United Nations Congress on the Prevention of Crime and the Treatment of Offenders. Available at: www.restorativejustice.org/resources/policy/inter/un/prosecutors. Accessed 9th December 2005.

United Nations Children's Fund (2009). Machel study 10-year strategic review: Children and conflict in a changing world. New York: Office of the Special Representative of the Secretary-General for Children and Armed Conflict, UNICEF. Available at: www.unicef.org/publications/files/Machel_Study_10_Year_Strategic_Review_EN_030909.pdf.

United Nations Convention on the Rights of the Child (1989). Convention on the Rights of the Child, A/RES/44/25 (20th November 1989). Available at: www.un.org/documents/ga/res/44/a44r025.htm.

United Nations Convention Relating to the Status of Refugees 1951 and the Protocol Relating to the Status of Refugees (1967) Article 1. Available at: www.ohchr.org/EN/ProfessionalInterest/Pages/CAT.aspx. Accessed 25th December 2015.

United Nations Declaration on Rights of the Child. Comment 6, Section 7.

United Nations General Assembly (2000). Optional Protocol to the Convention on the Rights of the Child on the Involvement of Children in Armed Conflict, 25th May 2000. Available at: www.refworld.org/docid/47fdfb180.html. Accessed 7th February 2014.

United Nations General Assembly (2000). Protocol to Prevent, Suppress and Punish Trafficking in Persons, Especially Women and Children, Supplementing the United Nations Convention against Transnational Organized Crime, 15th November 2000. Available at: www.refworld.org/docid/4720706c0.html. Accessed 7th February 2014.

United Nations General Assembly (2005). Convention on the Rights of the Child, Comment Three. Paragraph 21. June 3rd 2005. Available at: http://daccess-dds-ny.un.org/doc/UNDOC/GEN/G05/438/05/PDF/G0543805.pdf?OpenElement. Accessed 13th March 2013.

United Nations High Commissioner for Refugees (UNHCR). Speeches by António Guterres; Briefing on the Humanitarian Situation in Syria. New York, 21st December 2015. Available at: www.unhcr.org/search comid=42b2f01a4&cid=49aea93a4c&scid.

United Nations Relief and Works Agency for Palestine Refugees in the Near East. Available at: www.unrwa.org/palestine-refugees.

United Nations Security Council (2007). Report of the Secretary-General on children and armed conflict in the Sudan, UN Doc. S/2007/520, 29th August 2007. Available at: www.un.org/docs/sc/sgrep07.html.

Universal Declaration of Human Rights (1948). Article 3: Everyone has the right to life, liberty and security of person, Universal Declaration of Human Rights. Available at: www.un.org/en/documents/udhr/.

What to do if you're worried a child is being abused (2006)—Gov.uk.
    Available at: www.gov.uk/government/.../Archived-DFES-04320-
    2006-ChildAbuse.pdf.

Williams, R. (2008). British-born teenagers being trafficked for sexual exploi-
    tation within UK. *The Guardian, 3rd July 2008.* Available at: www.theguard-
    ian.com/society/2008/jul/03/childprotection.internationalcrime.

Wirtz, L. (2009). *Hidden Children: Separated Children at Risk.* London: The
    Children's Society. Available at: www.childrenssociety.org.uk/what-
    we-do/lobbying/policy-areas/young-refugees-and-migrants/hidden-
    children.

INDEX